# TREASURE

## LITERACY ACTIVITY BOOK

**Senior Authors**
J. David Cooper
John J. Pikulski

**Authors**
Kathryn H. Au
Margarita Calderón
Jacqueline C. Comas
Marjorie Y. Lipson
J. Sabrina Mims
Susan E. Page
Sheila W. Valencia
MaryEllen Vogt

**Consultants**
Dolores Malcolm
Tina Saldivar
Shane Templeton

INVITATIONS TO LITERACY

## Houghton Mifflin Company • Boston

Atlanta • Dallas • Geneva, Illinois • Palo Alto • Princeton

*Illustration Credits*

Elizabeth Allen iii, 5, 14, 17, 44, 52; Andrea Barrett 9, 10; Shirley Beckes 21, 31, 33; Ka Botzis/Melissa Turk 75, 77, 80; Cindy Brodie/Square Moon Productions 91; Ruth Brunke 32, 53, 73, 84; Jenny Campbell/Deborah Wolfe 54; Randy Chewning/HK Portfolio 12, 15, 19, 35, 37, 50, 123; Olivia Cole/Asciutto Art Reps 53, 56, 61, 68, 89, 93, 109; Mark Corcoran/Asciutto Art Reps 71, 72; Laura D'Argo iv, 43, 51, 83, 85, 96, 97, 100, 108, 111, 117, 120; Ruta Daugavietis 49, 81, 82; Susanne Demarco/Asciutto Art Reps 47; Darius Detwiler/Mendola 24; Shelly Dieterichs-Morrison 101, 104; Tom Duckworth 103; Kate Flanagan/Cornell & McCarthy 115; Bryan Friel/Steven Edsey 13, 22; Dave Garbot 3, 8; Robin Michal Koontz 67, 69; Bob Lange iii, 76, 84; Ruth Linstromberg 102, 107; Lynn Martin/Cliff Knecht 64, 65, 70; Deborah Morse/Square Moon Productions 107; Andy Myer/Deborah Wolfe 55, 58, 59; Jan Pyk/Asciutto Art Reps 95, 98; Miriam Sagasti 99, 105, 106; Sally Springer 114, 119, 122; Lynn Sweat/Cornell & McCarthy 88; Dave Winter 41, 48, 63.

*Photo Credits*

©Betts Anderson/Unicorn Stock Photos 23, right; ©W. Cody/Westlight 60; ©H. Armstrong Roberts, Inc. 38; ©Robert C. Hermes/ Photo Researchers, Inc. 79, top; ©Image Club Graphics, Inc. 24; ©PhotoDisc iv, 21, 34, 118 121; ©Rod Planck/Photo Researchers, Inc. 113; All other photographs by Ralph J. Brunke Photography.

ISBN: 0-395-74366-4

11 12 13 14 15-WC-00 99 98 97

# CONTENTS

# CONTENTS

## Consonant Sounds and Letters

Bb
bird

Cc
cat

Dd
dinosaur

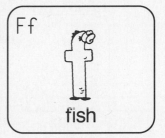
Ff
fish

Gg
ghost

Hh
horse

Jj
jack-in-the-box

Kk
king

Ll
lion

Mm
monster

Nn
nurse

Pp
pig

Qq
queen

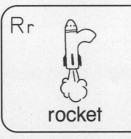
Rr
rocket

Ss
seal

Tt
tiger

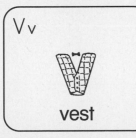
Vv
vest

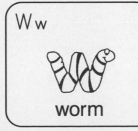
Ww
worm

Yy
yarn

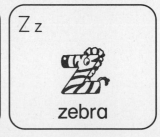
Zz
zebra

# MAGIC PICTURES

## Vowel Sounds and Letters

### A a

alligator

acorn

### E e

elephant

eel

### I i
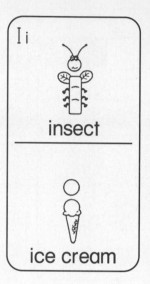
insect

ice cream

### O o

ostrich

ocean

### U u

umbrella

unicorn

# Let's Recycle It!

Help Harvey recycle. Cut out and paste the pictures
where they belong.

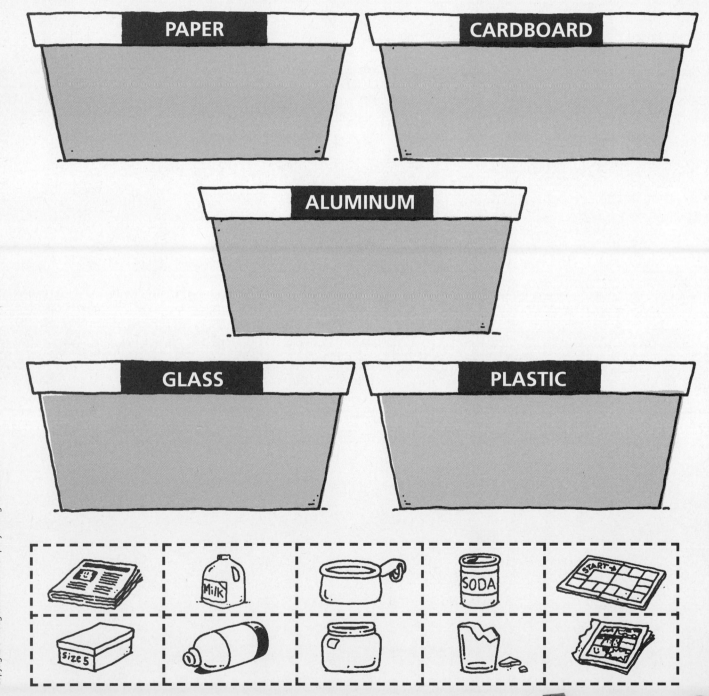

---

Name _____

Name

Clean Your Room, Harvey Moon!

**PHONICS/DECODING**
Vowel Pairs: *oo, ew, ue*

# Harvey Can Cook, Too

Finish the sentences with words from the box. Cut and paste the pictures that go with the sentences.

> cookies
> broom
> spoon
> stool
> newspaper
> glued

1. Harvey wants to make _____.

2. Sometimes he finds recipes in the _____.

3. His recipes are _____ Into a cookbook.

4. Everything is stirred together with a _____.

5. While the cookies bake, he waits on a _____.

**Family Photos** 5

Copyright © Houghton Mifflin Company. All rights reserved.

# Harvey's Garage Sale

**Help Harvey write price tags for the things he wants to sell. Use these words.**

clean

today

notice

few

shout

should

done

Don't _____

at your friends. Use this old

phone to call them.  $1

You _____ buy

this ball _____ .  25¢

Why not buy a _____

books? Then give them away when

you are _____

with them.  12 for 50¢

Be sure to  $1

_____ how

neat and _____

this used shirt is.

.......................................................

Name

# Make It Rhyme

Finish the poem about Harvey's cool
cat.  Write a sentence that rhymes
with each line below.

**Example:**
Remember me? I'm Harvey's cool cat.
I'm striped and furry and a little bit fat.

**1** I follow Harvey everywhere.

_____

**2** Harvey needs me when he cleans his room.

_____

**3** We work all day and don't even eat.

_____

**4** We clean the closet and under the bed, too.

_____

**5** And when at last we are all done,

_____

Name _____

# Begin with a Brainstorm

Plan your poem.

> **List some topics.  Circle the one you like best.**

> **What do you want to tell about?  Write your ideas.**

> **What are some rhyming words you might use?**

# Harvey's Cleanup

Each Spelling Word is spelled with the letters **oo**. These letters make two different vowel sounds.

the 🌙 vowel sound ➡ moon

the 📖 vowel sound ➡ book

## Spelling Words

1. **room**      5. **look**
2. **moon**      6. **noon**
3. **book**      7. **broom**
4. **soon**      8. **foot**

 **Your Own Words**

**Write the Spelling Words. Draw a line from each sock to the drawer that has the matching vowel sound.**

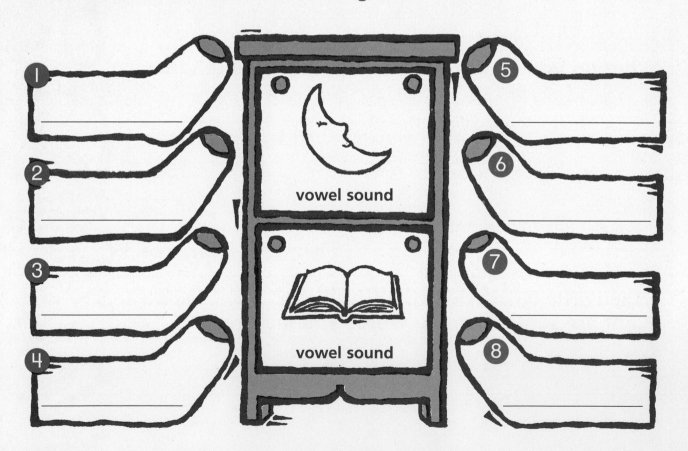

vowel sound

vowel sound

**Which two Spelling Words rhyme with cook?**

9 _____      10 _____

# Spelling Spree

### Spelling Words

1. **room**  5. **look**
2. **moon**  6. **noon**
3. **book**  7. **broom**
4. **soon**  8. **foot**

Write a Spelling Word for each clue.

1 part of your leg ___ ___ ___ ___

2 to see with your eyes ___ ___ ___ ___

3 a place with four walls ___ ___ ___ ___

4 It shines at night. ___ ___ ___ ___

5 You clean with this. ___ ___ ___ ___

**Where did Harvey put everything? Find out
by writing the letters in the boxes.**

Secret Word: ☐ ☐ ☐ ☐ ☐

**Find and circle three Spelling
Words that are spelled wrong in
this list. Then write each word
correctly.**

6 _____

7 _____

8 _____

**Things to Do Today**

•Eat breakfast as sone as you get up.

•Pick up the clothes in your room.

•Sweep the floor with a broom.

•Return library bok.

•Eat lunch at nune.

# Working Words

What if Harvey had a robot to help him clean his room!  Finish each sentence to show what Harvey tells his robot to do.

| cook | sweep |
|------|-------|
| wash | dust |
| walk | plant |

"You will _____!"

"You will _____!"

"You will _____!"

"You will _____!"

"You will _____!"

"You will _____!"

Name

# Tip the Piggy

**Answer the question or follow the directions.**

**1** Jenny brought home some tips from her new job. Circle the tips.

**2** Help Jenny count her money.

How many dollar bills? _____

How much change? _____

**3** Jenny puts her savings in her piggy bank. Draw four dollars in the bank.

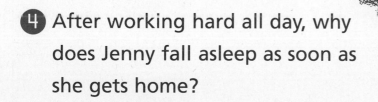

**4** After working hard all day, why does Jenny fall asleep as soon as she gets home?

_____

**5** When her bank gets full, Jenny wants to buy her mother the best present in the world. What do you think she will buy?

_____

**6** What would you buy?

_____

_____

Name

# Show and Tell

Write what each object is.

Tell what story event it makes you think about.

_____

_____

_____

_____

_____

_____

_____

_____

_____

_____

_____

_____

Name

# What's Next?

Cut and paste the pictures to show what happens.
Then finish each story with your own sentence.

1 _____

_____

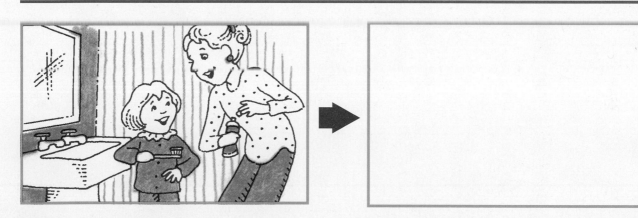

2 _____

_____

**Family Photos** 15

Name _____

# Start a Scrapbook

Write the words that have the same vowel sound as the picture name.

1. _____
2. _____
3. _____
4. _____

| | |
|---|---|
| arm | fall |
| far | first |
| girl | hard |
| shirt | small |
| start | wall |
| tall | third |

5. _____
6. _____
7. _____
8. _____

9. _____
10. _____
11. _____
12. _____

Name

# Thanks a Bunch!

Use these words to complete each sentence.  Then add today's date and finish the thank-you note.

| brought | buy | fall | four | full | world |

_____, 19_____

Dear Friends,

    My mother, my grandmother, and I want to thank you

for the food and furniture you _____

to our new apartment.  You're my best friends in the

whole _____.  The table and

_____ chairs look nice in our new kitchen.

Now, when our jar of money is _____,

we can _____ the big chair we are saving

for.  I hope we get a big one, so I can sit beside Mama when

I _____ asleep.

_____

_____

_____

_____

_____

_____

# Spend or Save?

Write the words from the box on the coins.  Then paste a word on each jar to make an opposite pair.

| | |
|---|---|
| new | sad |
| day | left |
| last | open |

**1** close

**2** right

**3** happy

**4** night

**5** old

**6** first

Write a sentence that uses the word pair from one jar.

_____

_____

Name

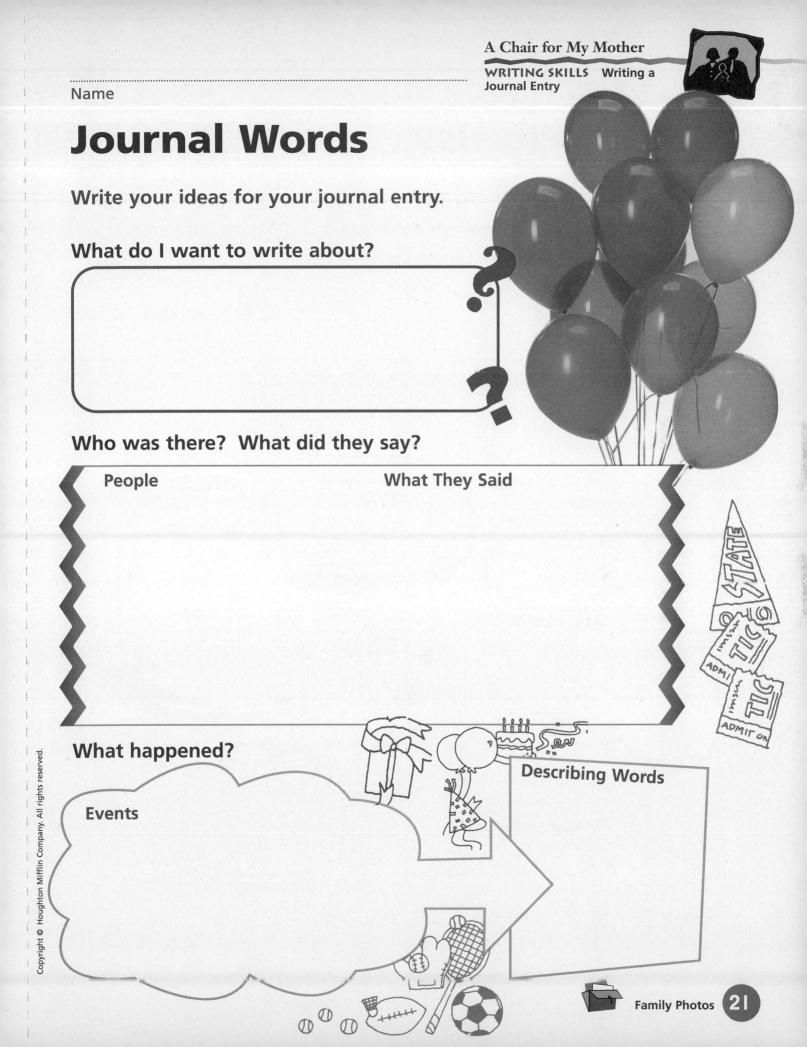

Name

# Journal Words

Write your ideas for your journal entry.

**What do I want to write about?**

**Who was there?  What did they say?**

| People | What They Said |
| --- | --- |
|  |  |

**What happened?**

Events

Describing Words

Name _____

# Jars of Words

Each Spelling Word has a vowel sound that is not short or long. It is the vowel sound that you hear in **car**. This vowel sound is different because the vowel is followed by **r**.

the vowel + r sound ➜ jar, arm

**Write the missing Spelling Words to finish each clue. Then draw a line under the letters that spell the vowel + r sound.**

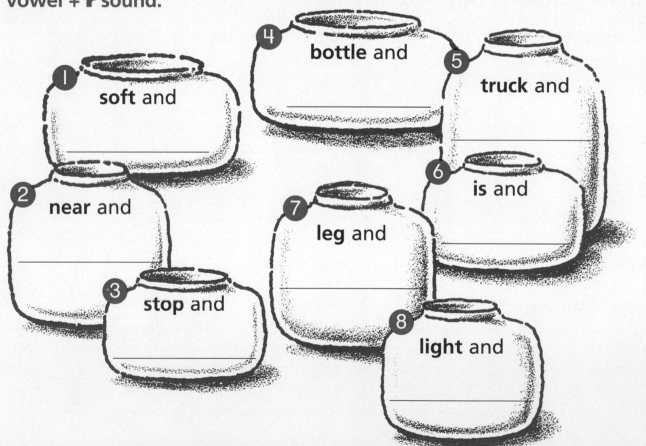

1. **soft** and _____

2. **near** and _____

3. **stop** and _____

4. **bottle** and _____

5. **truck** and _____

6. **is** and _____

7. **leg** and _____

8. **light** and _____

Which two Spelling Words begin with a vowel?

9. _____    10. _____

# Spelling Spree

A Chair for My Mother

SPELLING  The Vowel + r Sound in *car*

Name

# Spelling Spree

Spelling Words

| Spelling Words | |
|---|---|
| 1. jar | 5. start |
| 2. arm | 6. car |
| 3. hard | 7. far |
| 4. are | 8. dark |

Write a Spelling Word to finish the second sentence in each pair.

1. It is **light** outside during the **day**.
   It is ____ outside during the **night**.

2. A **pillow** is **soft**.
   A **rock** is ____.

3. Your **foot** is part of your **leg**.
   Your **hand** is part of your ____ .

4. A **bottle** has a **cap**.
   A ____ has a **lid**.

① _____

② _____

③ _____

④ _____

Find and circle four Spelling Words that are spelled wrong in this ad. Then write each word correctly.

## THE HOME STORE

Is your chair worn? Is the seat too hard? Buy a new one! Our chairs ar the best in town. A big sale will stard next week. The Home Store is not farr from the airport. Park your kar in our big lot.

⑤ _____

⑥ _____

⑦ _____

⑧ _____

Copyright © Houghton Mifflin Company. All rights reserved.

Family Photos **23**

# Spare Change

Make sentences by choosing a coin from each jar.
Remember to add **s** to a verb that tells about one.
Write each sentence correctly.

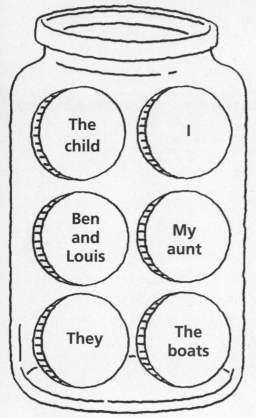
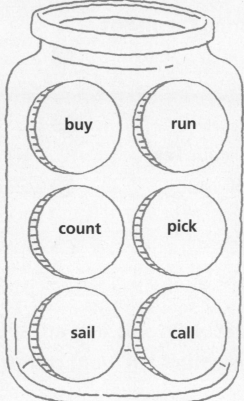
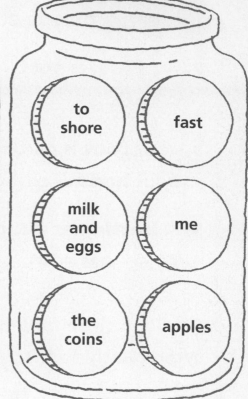

The child | I

Ben and Louis | My aunt

They | The boats

buy | run

count | pick

sail | call

to shore | fast

milk and eggs | me

the coins | apples

 1 _____

 2 _____

 3 _____

 4 _____

 5 _____

6 _____

Name

# Plan It!

**Draw pictures of what will happen in your story.**

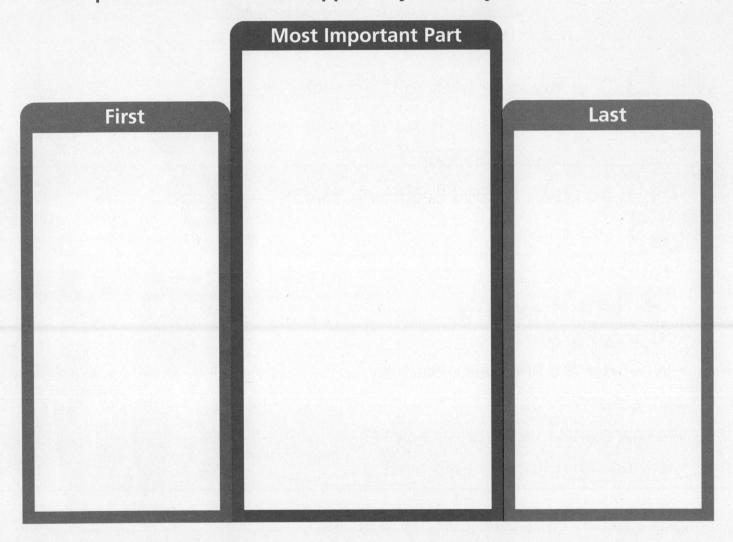

**Most Important Part**

**First**

**Last**

**Write some sentences to tell about your pictures.**

_____

_____

_____

_____

# Look Again

## • Revising Checklist •

Answer these questions about your true story.

- ☐ Does my story keep to the topic?
- ☐ Have I told enough so the reader can picture what happens?
- ☐ Do I have a good beginning, middle, and end?

## Questions to Ask My Writing Partner

- What do you like best about my true story?
- Is there anything that isn't clear?
- Is there anything I should add?

## How I Can Make My Story Better

_____

_____

_____

_____

_____

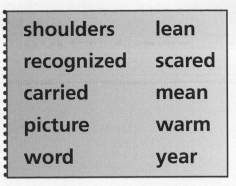

Name

# Step By Step

Finish this puzzle.  Use the word
that fits each clue.

| shoulders | lean |
| recognized | scared |
| carried | mean |
| picture | warm |
| word | year |

**Down**

1. parts of the body
2. afraid
3. to rest on something
4. something you take with a camera
7. a group of letters
8. "I didn't ____ to do it!"

**Across**

5. held something and took it somewhere
6. knew who someone was
7. not cool
9. twelve months

# Bobby's Photo Album

Complete each sentence in the album.  Draw a picture to go with each sentence.

When Bobby was a baby,

_____

_____

When Bobby was

growing up, _____

_____

On Bobby's fifth birthday,

_____

_____

When Bob went to the

hospital, _____

_____

Name _____

# Bobby's Diary

Cut out and paste the notes in Bobby's diary in the order that they happened.

**Bob came home today.**

_____

_____

_____

_____

Bob walked to the end of the lawn.

Bob smiled a little when I made a tower with blocks.

Bob doesn't remember me.

Bob leaned on me and started to walk.

30

# Find the Hidden Word

Write a word from the box to fit each clue.

| | |
|---|---|
| core | shore |
| torn | corn |
| sport | worn |

**1** ripped ☐ __ __ __ __

**2** eat it on the cob __ ☐ __ __

**3** what was done with a shirt __ ☐ __ __

**4** center of an apple __ __ __ ☐

**5** land next to a lake __ __ ☐ __ __

**6** game such as baseball ☐ __ __ __ __

**Now write the letters from the boxes to make a word that finishes the sentence.**

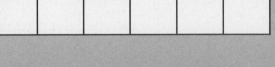

**7** Bob and Bobby made ☐☐☐☐☐☐.

Name _____

# Sign Makers

Help get the amusement park ready for Bob
and Bobby's visit.  Write a word from a
balloon to finish each sign.

carried
warm · year
picture · mean · word

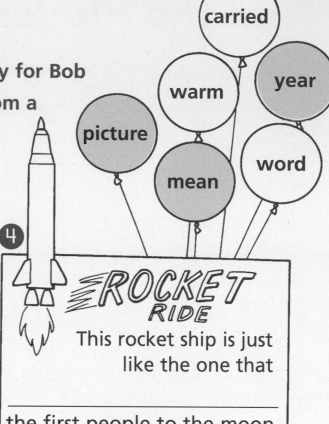

**1**  Get your

_____

taken here!

**2**  HOT FOOD

Are you cold?  You can

_____ up here.

**4**  ROCKET RIDE

This rocket ship is just
like the one that

_____

the first people to the moon.

**5**  MONSTER ROLLER COASTER

We don't _____
to scare you, but it is
a long way down!

**3**  DARTS

ball fish bear ring bear fish ball

Hit the

_____

and win a prize.

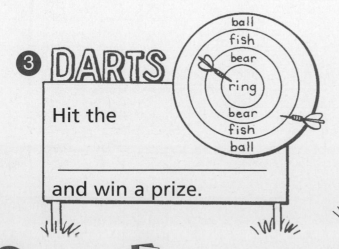

**6**  I will guess the

_____

you were born.

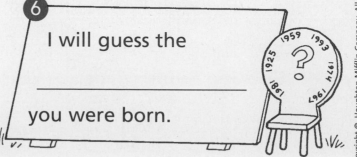

Name

# How Many Syllables?

How many parts does each word have?  Write the
word next to the block that tells the number of parts.

| better | hospital | talk | monster | sneeze |
| tower | spoon | shoulders | slowly | grandfather |

**1**

**2**

**2**

**2**

**3**

**1**

**1**

**2**

**2**

**3**

Use two words from the box in a sentence of your own. Circle all
the words with one syllable and underline all the words with two.

_____

_____

# Together Again

Write about a special day for Bob and
Bobby. Use verbs from the box.
Draw a picture to show what happens.

grabbed
shouted
glided
danced
gulped
romped
studied
tiptoed

Name

# Step by Step

Each Spelling Word has the vowel + **r** sound that you hear in **store**. This sound is often spelled **or** or **ore**.

the vowel + r sound → for, more

## Spelling Words

1. **for**
2. **more**
3. **or**
4. **story**
5. **born**
6. **short**
7. **store**
8. **corn**

Your Own Words

Write the Spelling Words. Color orange each word in which the vowel + **r** sound is spelled **or**. Color yellow each word in which the vowel + **r** sound is spelled **ore**.

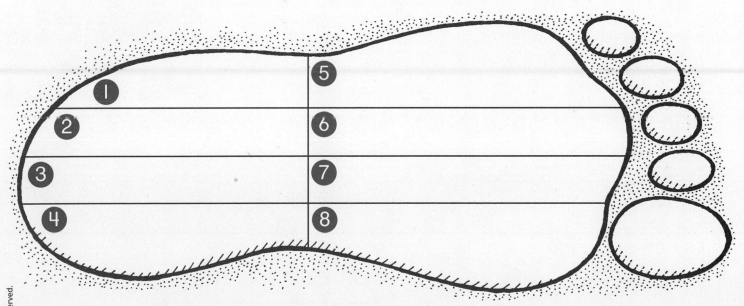

1 _____
2 _____
3 _____
4 _____
5 _____
6 _____
7 _____
8 _____

Write Spelling Words to answer the questions.

9 Which word begins with the **sh** sound? _____

10 Which word begins and ends like **barn**? _____

# Spelling Spree

Write the Spelling Word that matches
each clue.

**1** a shop　　　　　　_____

**2** a newly ____ baby　_____

**3** a vegetable　　　_____

**4** a tale　　　　　　_____

**5** tall or ____　　　_____

Find and circle three Spelling Words that are spelled wrong
in these get-well cards. Then write each word correctly.

I miss you mor
every day.
Get better so
we can play.

This short poem
is just fer you.
Get well soon
orr I will be blue.

**6** _____

**7** _____

**8** _____

**GRAMMAR** Verbs with -ed

# All in the Past

Use the clues to write a verb that tells about the past. Use the words in the box to help you.

| talk | miss |
|------|------|
| jump | look |
| trick | brush |
| play | walk |

1 cleaned the teeth

___ ___ ___ ___ [ ] ___ ___

2 watched

___ [ ] ___ ___ ___ ___

3 didn't catch the bus

___ ___ ___ [ ] ___ ___

4 leaped

___ ___ ___ [ ] ___

5 fooled someone

___ ___ [ ] ___ ___ ___

6 spoke

[ ] ___ ___ ___ ___

7 had fun

___ ___ [ ] ___ ___

8 went by foot

___ ___ [ ] ___ ___

Answer the question by writing the boxed letters.

Where did Bob go when he was sick?

[ ] [ ] [ ] [ ] [ ] [ ] [ ] [ ]

**Family Photos** 37

Name _____

# The Ring's the Thing

**Follow the rhyme trail and complete the rhymes.**

| nearly   shock   second   light   confess |

**1**
My ring looked white

In the bright _____.

**5**
Had someone, somewhere
Swallowed my ring?

**2**
Had I put it there?
I couldn't find it anywhere.

**6**
Wait a _____,
Who would do such a thing?

**3**
It was a _____
Not to find it by the clock.

**7**
I had to _____
This was such a mess.

**4**
Where could a ring hide?

I _____ cried.

**8**
"Let me interrupt you," Mother said.
"Look what is here by the book
    that I read."

**9**
I had to laugh.  I began to sing.
After all, I did not lose the ring!

Name

# Tamale Test!

Circle **True** or **Not True**.

**1** Maria made tamales by herself.                                    True       Not True

**2** Maria was unhappy about making tamales.              True       Not True

**3** Maria wanted to try on the diamond ring.              True       Not True

**4** Maria's mother never took off the ring.                  True       Not True

**5** Maria was worried when the ring was missing.      True       Not True

**6** Maria thought the ring fell into the trash.             True       Not True

**7** Maria and her cousins ate all the tamales.            True       Not True

**8** They found the ring in the last tamale.                 True       Not True

**9** Maria's mother was angry that Maria had
played with her diamond ring.                                      True       Not True

**10** Maria's whole family made a second batch
of tamales.                                                                      True       Not True

**Choose two sentences that are not true. On the back of this paper, rewrite each sentence to make it true.**

**Rewrite two sentences to make them true.**

_____

_____

_____

_____

_____

_____

........................................................................
Name

# Story Chain

Write a story part in each box.  Make a
chain by gluing the boxes in order.  Write
your name in the title box.

TOO MANY TAMALES

**Retold by:** _____

| Glue here | **Setting:** |
|---|---|

| Glue here | **Event:** |
|---|---|

| Glue here | **Main Characters:** |
|---|---|

| Glue here | **Event:** |
|---|---|

| Glue here | **Problem:** |
|---|---|

| Glue here | **Event:** |
|---|---|

| Glue here | **Event:** |
|---|---|

| Glue here | **Ending:** |
|---|---|

**Use the story chain to retell the story to a partner.**

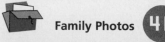

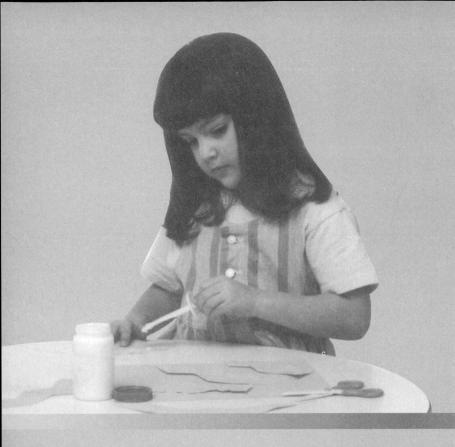

Name

Too Many Tamales

**PHONICS/DECODING** Base
Words and Prefixes: *re-, dis-, un-*

# Tips for Tamales

Write a word beginning on each line to complete the
word that best fits the tip.

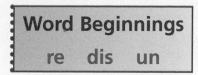

**Word Beginnings**
re   dis   un

1  You will need to _____heat the tamale if it cools

a little.

2  If you are _____able to take off the corn husk,

ask for help.

3  You can save the husks and _____use them the

next time you make tamales.

4  Don't _____wrap the filling.

5  If you _____like the taste at first, don't give up

on this special food.

Write your own tamale tip using a word with **re**, **dis**,
or **un**.

_____

_____

Copyright © Houghton Mifflin Company. All rights reserved.

Family Photos  43

Name

# Maria's Family Album

Write a word to complete each sentence. Then draw
a line between the base word and ending of the
word you wrote.

| taller | opened | fastest | laughed | drinking |

1. Teresa is _____ milk.

2. Maria is the _____ runner.

3. Maria is _____ than Teresa.

4. Teresa _____ a gift.

5. We _____ at the funny story.

# A Recipe for Fun

**Cut out the words at the bottom of the page.**
**Paste the words in the boxes to**
**finish the recipe.**

## Toast Treats

**1** Pour a little milk into four glasses. Use [ ] milk, not

chocolate or strawberry.

**2** Add a few drops of food coloring to each glass. In the first

glass, add red. In the [ ] glass, add blue. In the

third, add yellow. In the last, add green.

**3** Put the bread in the toaster until it is [ ] brown, not

dark brown.

**4** Paint a picture on the toast with the colored milk.

**5** Toast the bread again. Have a grown-up check the toast when

you think it's [ ] done. The picture won't show if the

toast gets burned.

**6** Does the picture make you smile or [ ]? Make a

Toast Treat for someone else and make them happy, too!

**Now cut out the recipe card. You might try this recipe at home.**

| second | laugh | white | light | nearly |

Name

Too Many Tamales

**VOCABULARY**  Words with
the Suffix *-ful*

# Helpful Cooks

Everyone can help make tamales.  Write
a sentence for each picture.  Use a word
from the box in each sentence.

| armful | cupful |
|--------|--------|
| handful | mouthful |

① _____

_____

③ _____

_____

② _____

_____

④ _____

_____

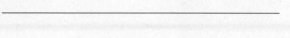

Name

# Let's Eat Out

**Look at the picture. Write complete sentences about what is happening. You might use words from the box.**

| laughing | throwing | eating | talking | happy |
|---|---|---|---|---|
| hungry | family | baby | father | boy |

_____

_____

_____

_____

_____

_____

Name

# Crossword House

Each Spelling Word has the vowel + **r** sound that you hear at the end of . This sound is often spelled **er**.

the vowel + **r** sound ➜ better, after

**Write a Spelling Word for each clue in the puzzle.  Then color the squares that have the letters that spell the vowel + r sound.**

## Spelling Words

| | |
|---|---|
| 1. **better** | 5. **mother** |
| 2. **after** | 6. **father** |
| 3. **over** | 7. **sister** |
| 4. **under** | 8. **brother** |

**Your Own Words**

**Across**

3. a woman in
   a family

4. a girl in a family

5. a man in a family

7. good, _____, best

8. below

**Down**

1. a boy in a family

2. above

6. before and _____

**Write Spelling Words to answer the questions.**

9. Which word begins like **monster**? _____

10. Which word begins like **seed**? _____

# Spelling Spree

Write a Spelling Word to name each person in this family tree.

| Spelling Words | |
|---|---|
| 1. **better** | 5. **mother** |
| 2. **after** | 6. **father** |
| 3. **over** | 7. **sister** |
| 4. **under** | 8. **brother** |

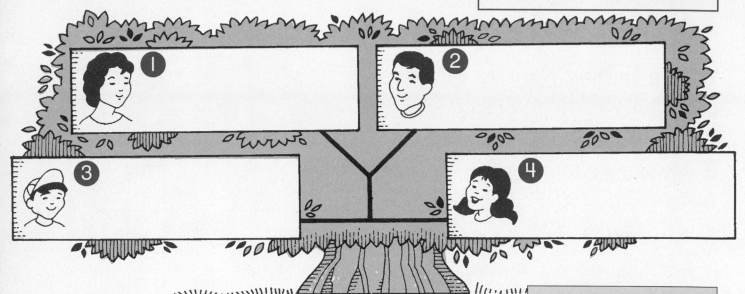

Find and circle four Spelling Words that are spelled wrong in this recipe. Then write each word correctly.

5. _____

6. _____

7. _____

8. _____

## TAMALE PIE

Follow these steps to make a tamale pie.

◆ Add 1 cup of cornmeal to 4 cups of water and cook for 45 minutes.

◆ Spread the mix in a pan aftur you grease it.

◆ Spread tomatoes and meat ovr the mix. Red tomatoes are beter than green ones.

◆ Brown the tamales undar the broiler.

Have your mother or father try this tasty dish!

# To Be or Not to Be

**Write sentences to answer the questions about the picture.**

**1** Who is very hungry?

_____

**2** Where were the vegetables?

_____

**3** How many places are there at the table?

_____

**4** Where was the puppy?

_____

**Write your own sentence about the picture.**
**Use is, are, was, or were.**

_____

_____

Name

# Late Again!

Mia has a big problem. She needs her family's help to solve
it. So Mia taped this note to the kitchen cupboard.

Dear Family,

    I was late to school again today! I fell back asleep after
Mom woke me up. Then I got dressed in a hurry, but my socks
didn't match. Uncle Joe made me change them. Next, Grandma
gave me a huge bowl of oatmeal. She made me eat all of it. Then
I had to wait for Frank to get out of the bathroom. I ran to
school. But I was still late, and my teacher was upset.

    Please think of a way to help me be on time tomorrow!

            Love,

            Mia

## Make a Story Cartoon

Make a story cartoon that tells what
Mia's family will do
tomorrow to help
Mia get to school
on time. Use a
separate sheet of
paper to write
down your ideas
in story order.

## Cartoon Checklist

- [ ] My pictures show how Mia's family helped her.

- [ ] I have drawn my pictures in story order.

- [ ] I can explain my cartoon clearly to others.

Name

# Tales and Details

Read the ad about a lost boa constrictor and complete the chart.

**MISSING**

Please help me find my boa constrictor! It is brown with large and small tan spots. It is 12 feet long and likes to meet animals. It was last seen on a farm with a large load of wash. It was crawling through a pair of blue jeans and swallowing a white shirt.

**Details About the Boa**

_____

_____

_____

_____

_____

_____

_____

That's Incredible!   **53**

# Bye-Bye, Boa

Read each sentence and look at the picture.  Choose the
word that goes with the sentence and write it on the line.
Then underline the base word in the word you wrote.

| running   spotted   mopping   lunches   pigs |

**1** A minute ago, the farmer

_____

the snake in the hen house.

**2** The farmer is _____
to the hen house.

**3** Now he  is _____
up the mess in the hen house.

**4** Meanwhile, the _____
are in the school bus.

**5** They are eating all the children's

_____ .

   That's Incredible!

# Coming Soon

Use words from the box to complete the movie ad. Then draw a picture showing your favorite scene from the movie.

| | |
|---|---|
| class | farm |
| finally | sound |
| egg | hurry |

## THE DAY JIMMY'S BOA ATE THE WASH

The movie you've waited for is

_____

at a theater near you!

Mrs. Stanley's second-grade

_____

has a day they will never forget. It all
begins with a simple trip to a

_____ .

If that doesn't _____ exciting, just wait!
You won't believe what happens when a hen lays an

_____ .

What does all this have to do with a boa that ate the wash? If you

want to find out, _____ to the theater.
You'll be glad you did!

That's Incredible!  55

Name

# Sounds Alike

**Follow the directions to complete the picture.**

**1** Draw two **pairs** of **pears** in the tree.

**2** Next **to** the flower, draw **two** bees.

**3** Look **for** the kittens.  Draw **four** bowls of milk near them.

**4** Circle the chipmunk's **hole**.  Color the **whole** watermelon green.

**Write a sentence about the picture.**

**Use one or more of the words in dark type.**

_____

_____

Name

# One Thing After Another

Fix Jimmy's letter. Cross out the underlined words.
Write **He, She, It**, or **They** above the words you
crossed out.

Dear Rick,

My class went to a farm. I brought my boa along.

My boa got away! My boa went into the hen house. The hens

went wild. The hens flew all over. The farmer tried to catch

them. The farmer did not have much luck.

Then a chicken dropped an egg on Jenny's head. Jenny was

very mad. Jenny threw an egg at Tommy. Tommy ducked. The

egg hit Marianne! The egg dripped all over her hair. Her hair

was a mess!

The farmer and his wife were mad. The farmer and his wife

may never ask us back.

Your friend,

Jimmy

 That's Incredible! **57**

Name

# Laundry for Lunch

Each Spelling Word names more than one
of something.  The **s** and **es** endings
make these words mean more than one.

Add **s** to most words to name more than
one.  Add **es** to words that end with **s**, **x**,
**sh**, or **ch** to name more than one.

s   ➜  trips, eggs
es  ➜  bu<u>s</u>es, bo<u>x</u>es, wi<u>sh</u>es, pea<u>ch</u>es

| Spelling Words | |
|---|---|
| 1. **trips** | 5. **wishes** |
| 2. **buses** | 6. **boxes** |
| 3. **classes** | 7. **games** |
| 4. **eggs** | 8. **peaches** |

**Your Own Words**

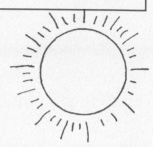

**Add s or es to the words hanging from the clothesline**
**to make Spelling Words.  Write the words you made.**

s                                                                    **es**

egg      peach   game      bus                    box      trip

class                              wish

s

**1** _____
**2** _____
**3** _____

es

**4** _____     **7** _____
**5** _____     **8** _____
**6** _____

**Which two Spelling Words begin with a consonant cluster?**

**9** _____     **10** _____

# Spelling Spree

Think how the words in each group are alike.  Write the missing Spelling Words.

<table>
<tr><td colspan="2">**Spelling Words**</td></tr>
<tr><td>1. **trips**</td><td>5. **wishes**</td></tr>
<tr><td>2. **buses**</td><td>6. **boxes**</td></tr>
<tr><td>3. **classes**</td><td>7. **games**</td></tr>
<tr><td>4. **eggs**</td><td>8. **peaches**</td></tr>
</table>

1. cars, trucks, ____

2. apples, pears, ____

3. milk, butter, ____

4. crate, cartons, ____

**1** _____   **3** _____

**2** _____   **4** _____

Find and circle four Spelling Words that are spelled wrong in this notice.  Then write each word correctly.

To:  All Students _____

From:  The Principal _____

   Your wishiz have come true!
On Friday, we will take the first of
many field tripps this year.  All
klasses will meet in front of the
school.  You may play gaims on the
buses, but please do not stand up.

**5** _____

**6** _____

**7** _____

**8** _____

..................................................
Name

# Those Are the Breaks!

Jenny and Sid are remembering their trip to the farm,
but they don't know which verbs to use.  Write the
verbs that tell about the past.  Then write an ending
for the story.  Use a verb that tells about the past.

**Jenny:**  The trip to the farm last week was so much fun!

I (throw, threw) _____ an egg at the side of the barn.

**Sid:**  You did?  What happened?

**Jenny:**  It (break, broke) _____ and made an awful

mess.  Don't you remember?

**Sid:**  No, I (take, took) _____ a nap on the bus.

The trip (make, made) _____ me sleepy.  What

happened next?

**Jenny:**  The teacher (make, made) _____ me

clean it up.

_____

_____

_____

Name _____

# What's Up, Dinosaur?

Finish each sentence by writing the correct word from the box. Then cut out the pieces and put them together.

cold
leave
bored
often
guess
invented
later

I _____ think about dinosaurs.

Scientists _____ ways to tell how old dinosaur bones are.

The earth may have become too _____ for the dinosaurs.

I can _____ what made dinosaurs extinct.

I read about dinosaurs.

Whenever I am _____

Once there were many of them, but _____ there were none.

Why did the dinosaurs _____ the earth?

Name _____

# A Dinosaur's Tale

**Imagine you are a dinosaur visiting Earth.
You are on a talk show. Answer the questions.**

How did you get along with people on Earth?

❶ _____
_____

How did people get cars, houses, and airplanes?

❷ _____
_____

If you did all those things for people, what did people do?

❸ _____
_____

Why did you leave Earth? How did you leave?

❹ _____
_____

**What else would you like to tell?**

_____
_____

Name

# Really? Not Really!

Write **real** if the picture shows something that could happen in real life. Write **fantasy** if the picture shows something that could happen only in a fantasy story.

_____        _____

_____        _____

Write a sentence about something that could happen in real life.

_____

_____

Write a sentence about something that could happen only in a fantasy story.

_____

_____

Name

# Scrambled Eggs

Cut and paste the eggs onto the nests to complete the sentences.
Be sure that the completed sentences make sense and
that they rhyme.

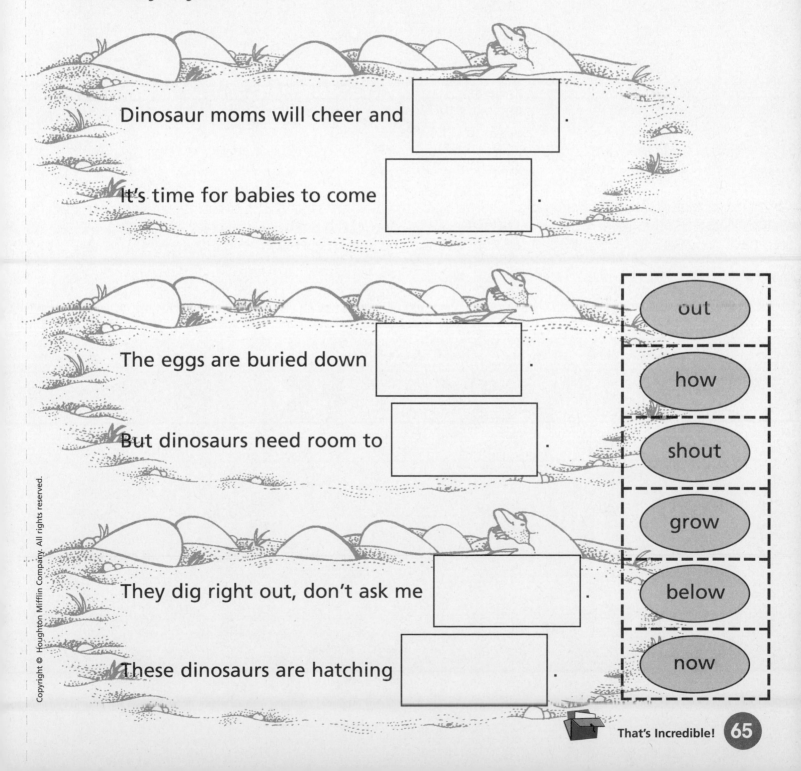

Dinosaur moms will cheer and _____ .

It's time for babies to come _____ .

The eggs are buried down _____ .

But dinosaurs need room to _____ .

They dig right out, don't ask me _____ .

These dinosaurs are hatching _____ .

out

how

shout

grow

below

now

That's Incredible! **65**

Name

# Dinosaur Bones

**Write each word next to its definition.**

| cold | guess | later | leave | often |
|------|-------|-------|-------|-------|

1. Many times. _____

2. Not warm or hot. _____

3. A time after now. _____

4. To try to think of an answer.

   _____

5. To go away from a place.

   _____

**Write sentences about dinosaurs, using at least three words that you wrote.**

_____

_____

_____

_____

...................................................
Name

# A Dinosaur's Circus

Look at the picture. Use a word in the box plus **'s** to complete each sentence. The first one has been done for you.

| boy |
| dinosaur |
| girl |
| bicycle |
| clown |

**Example:**

Look! There is a boy riding on a <u>dinosaur's</u> tail!

**1** The _____ hat is as tall as the roof.

**2** That _____ costume matches the dinosaur.

**3** The _____ shoes are big and silly.

**4** The _____ wheel is bigger than the dinosaur riding it.

**Write two sentences about the scene. Use some words with 's.**

**5** _____

_____

**6** _____

Name

# Here's Why!

Imagine that a dinosaur showed up in your back yard.  Write some reasons to persuade your family to let you keep it.

**Reason 1**

**Reason 2**

**Reason 3**

That's Incredible!   69

Name

# Dino Doings

Each Spelling Word has the vowel sound that you hear in  . This vowel sound may be spelled **ow** or **ou**.

the  vowel sound ➡ how, out

| Spelling Words | |
|---|---|
| 1. **how** | 5. **down** |
| 2. **out** | 6. **brown** |
| 3. **now** | 7. **cow** |
| 4. **house** | 8. **mouse** |

✎ Your Own Words

Write the missing letters to make Spelling Words. Then write the words under the matching spelling for the vowel sound in 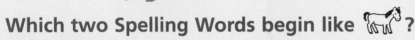 .

```
        m
      c _
  h _ _ s e
          e
b r _ _ n
    d _ _ n
        t
```

**ou**

1. _____

2. _____

3. _____

**ow**

4. _____

5. _____

6. _____

7. _____

8. _____

Which two Spelling Words begin like  ?

9. _____          10. _____

70  That's Incredible!

Name

# Spelling Spree

Each missing letter fits in ABC order between the other letters.  Write the missing letters.  Then use the missing letters to write the Spelling Words.

| Spelling Words | |
| --- | --- |
| 1. **how** | 5. **down** |
| 2. **out** | 6. **brown** |
| 3. **now** | 7. **cow** |
| 4. **house** | 8. **mouse** |

**Example:**  n __o__ p   t __u__ v   s __t__ u   **out**

1. m ___ o   n ___ p   v ___ x

2. a ___ c   q ___ s   n ___ p   v ___ x   m ___ o

3. g ___ i   n ___ p   v ___ x

4. l ___ n   n ___ p   t ___ v   r ___ t   d ___ f

5. b ___ d   n ___ p   v ___ x

❶ _____          ❹ _____

❷ _____          ❺ _____

❸ _____

Find and circle three Spelling Words that are spelled wrong on these signs. Then write each word correctly.

**6.** New Hous Now Being Built

**7.** Slow Doun! Workers Ahead

**8.** Watch Owt! Dinosaurs At Work

❻ _____

❼ _____

❽ _____

That's Incredible!   **71**

Name

# Riddle Time

Write the contraction that is the opposite of the word in **dark print** to finish each riddle. Then answer each riddle.

1. Sharks **did**, but most dinosaurs

   _____.

   _____

2. A frog **can**, but a dog

   _____.

   _____

3. A bird **does**, but a cat

   _____.

   _____

4. My parrot **could**, but my gerbil

   _____.

   _____

5. Monkeys **can**, but whales

   _____.

   _____

Now write your own riddle.

_____

_____

# Putting It Together

Cut out the definition puzzle pieces. Match each definition to the correct word. Paste the puzzle piece in the space.

What does the picture show? _____

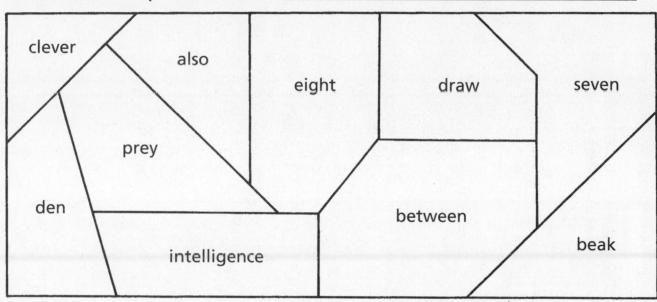

| | | | | |
|---|---|---|---|---|
| clever | also | eight | draw | seven |
| prey | | | | |
| den | | between | | |
| | intelligence | | | beak |

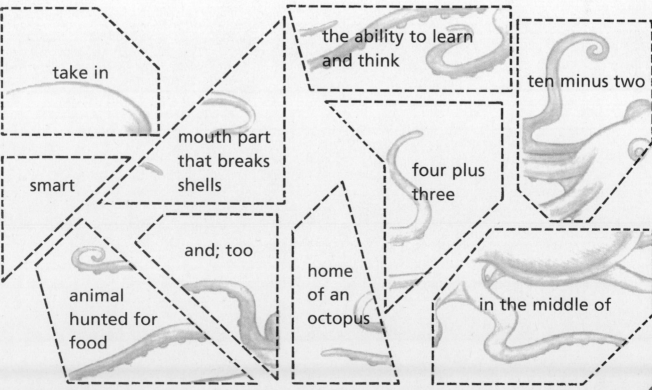

take in

the ability to learn and think

ten minus two

mouth part that breaks shells

smart

four plus three

and; too

home of an octopus

in the middle of

animal hunted for food

Name _____

# It's Amazing!

**Write words in the blanks to finish the newspaper article.**

New Facts About the _____

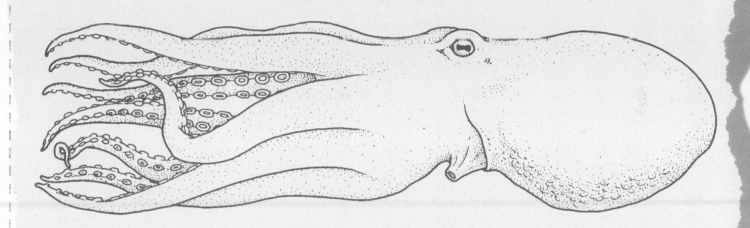

People have found out many facts about the octopus. Every octopus lives _____ in a den. An octopus can change _____ to match its surroundings. It can catch and hold food with the _____ on its arms.

An octopus can jet through the sea by drawing in _____ and shooting it out through its siphon. If an enemy tears off an octopus's arm, the arm _____. A female octopus weaves strings of _____ and hangs them in her den.

Octopuses also show signs of _____ by being able to solve problems. Really, an octopus is amazing!

Name ................................................

# Fact or Opinion?

Write **Fact** if the sentence can be proved.  Write **Opinion** if the sentence tells what someone feels or believes.

**1** An octopus spends its life alone. _____

**2** It would be very lonely to be an octopus. _____

**3** An octopus has no backbone. _____

**4** I believe that the blue-ringed octopus is the most beautiful

octopus of all. _____

**5** I don't think I would ever like to see an octopus swimming next

to me. _____

**6** An octopus eats crabs and lobsters. _____

**Now write one fact and one opinion about an octopus.**

**7** Fact:_____

_____

_____

**8** Opinion: _____

_____

_____

# Attach the Tentacles

Cut and paste endings to make words.  On the back of this paper, write sentences using three of the words you made.

**Example:**

hope **ful**

most

dirt

friend

ill

play

humor

y

ful

ous

ly

ness

ly

**Write sentences using three of the words you made.**

1. _____

   _____

2. _____

   _____

3. _____

   _____

Name _____

# The Amazing Octopus

Write the words that make sense in the sentences.

| almost | small | crawl | drawing |

**1** An octopus was born. It was very _____.

**2** For a month, the baby octopus could not swim

or _____.

**3** The octopus learned to swim by _____

in water and squirting it out.

**4** Soon it was _____ strong enough to open a

clam.

Write four sentences of your own about an octopus.
Use one word from the box in each sentence.

| draw | raw | also | saw |
|------|-----|------|-----|
| small | always | crawl | talk |

**5** _____

**6** _____

**7** _____

**8** _____

That's Incredible! 79

Name

# Label the Diagram

Read the words in the box. Use the words to complete the labels on the diagram.

| also | between |
| draw | eight |
| seven | |

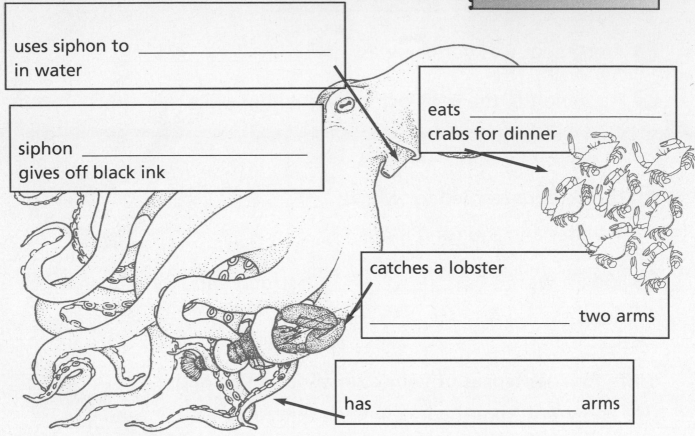

uses siphon to _____ in water

siphon _____ gives off black ink

eats _____ crabs for dinner

catches a lobster

_____ two arms

has _____ arms

Write a few sentences about the diagram. Use some words from the box.

_____

_____

_____

_____

Name _____

# Find the Meanings

Read the words and their definitions.  Then decide which
definition fits each sentence.  Write the correct definition.

| | | | | |
|---|---|---|---|---|
| **leaves** | 1. Goes away from. | **store** | 1. A place to buy things. |
| | 2. Parts of a plant. | | 2. To keep for later use. |
| **show** | 1. A performance. | | |
| | 2. To demonstrate. | | |

**1** An octopus **leaves** its den to hunt for food.

_____

**2** The **leaves** on the tree are green.

_____

**3** An octopus can **show** how it feels by changing color.

_____

**4** The seals put on a great **show** at the aquarium.

_____

**5** Sometimes octopuses **store** crabs in their suckers to eat later.

_____

**6** Did you buy anything at the fish **store**?

_____

On a separate sheet of paper, draw a picture showing one of the
meanings of **leaves, show,** or **store.**  See if a partner can guess
which meaning you drew.

That's Incredible!  **81**

Name

# What I See

**Imagine you are a scientist visiting an aquarium. You are watching an octopus and some other sea creatures. Write about what you see first, next, and last.**

## First

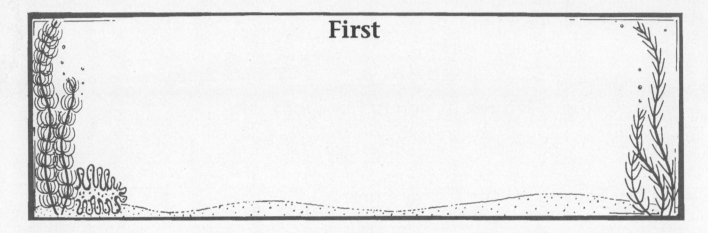

## Next

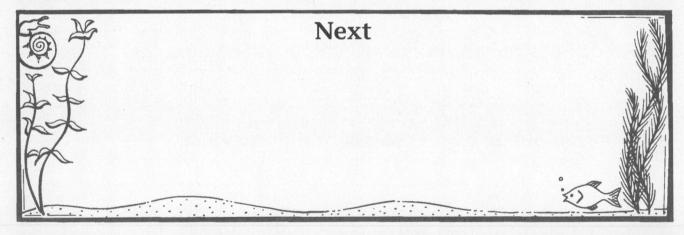

## Last

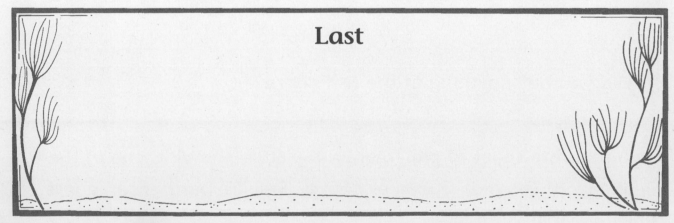

# Simply Amazing

Each Spelling Word has the vowel sound that you hear in . This vowel sound may be spelled **aw** or **a** before **ll**.

the  vowel sound ➜ draw,  all

Write the missing letters to make Spelling Words. Then write the words on the rock that has the matching spelling for the vowel sound in .

<table>
<tr><td>Spelling Words</td></tr>
</table>

**Spelling Words**

| | |
|---|---|
| 1. **all** | 5. **small** |
| 2. **call** | 6. **ball** |
| 3. **draw** | 7. **fall** |
| 4. **saw** | 8. **paw** |

Your Own Words

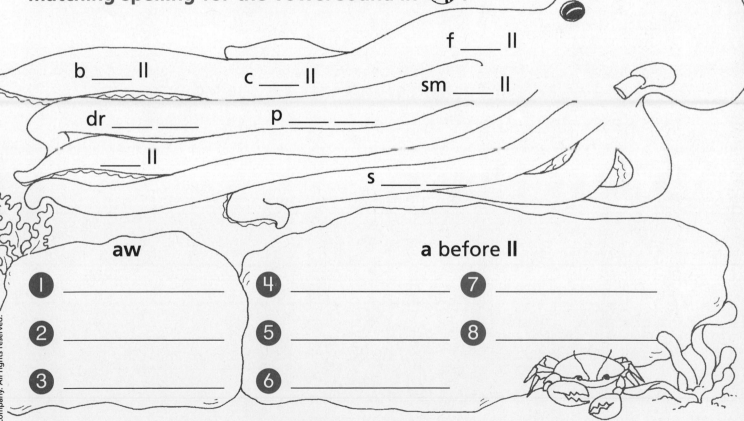

f ___ ll

b ___ ll          c ___ ll          sm ___ ll

dr ___ ___          p ___ ___

___ ll

s ___ ___

aw                                    **a** before **ll**

1 _____     4 _____     7 _____

2 _____     5 _____     8 _____

3 _____     6 _____

**Write Spelling Words to answer the questions.**

9 Which word begins like **pet**? _____

10 Which word begins like **dress**? _____

That's Incredible!  83

**Name** _____

# Spelling Spree

| Spelling Words | |
|---|---|
| 1. **all** | 5. **small** |
| 2. **call** | 6. **ball** |
| 3. **draw** | 7. **fall** |
| 4. **saw** | 8. **paw** |

**Write the word that goes with each clue.**

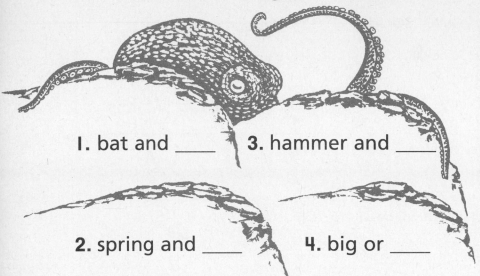

**1.** bat and ____        **3.** hammer and ____

**2.** spring and ____        **4.** big or ____

**1** _____

**2** _____

**3** _____

**4** _____

**Find and circle four Spelling Words that are spelled wrong in this news story. Then write each word correctly.**

# Class News

### My Diving Trip

On Tuesday my mother got a cal from my uncle. He asked us awl to go diving. We had a good time. I saw a baby octopus. It was only the size of a cat's pau. My uncle asked me to drow a picture of it. Here it is.

**5** _____

**6** _____

**7** _____

**8** _____

# The Sea Around Us

Find the picture that each sentence tells about. Then write the verb from that picture to complete the sentence correctly.

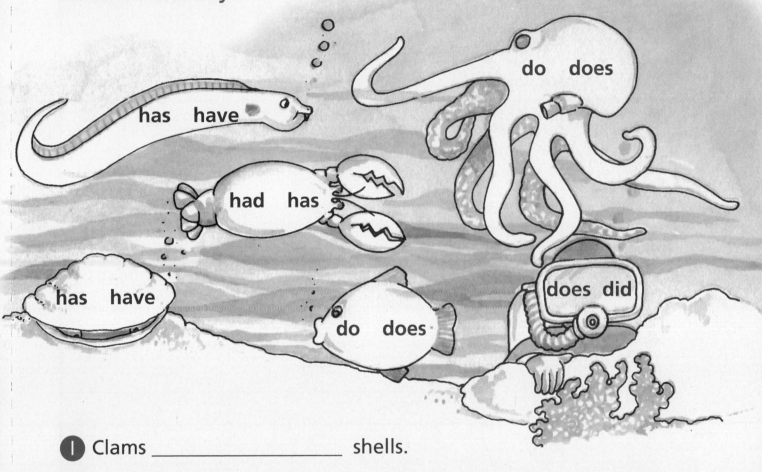

**1** Clams _____ shells.

**2** A moray eel _____ sharp teeth.

**3** Yesterday the lobster _____ a good meal.

**4** An octopus _____ amazing things.

**5** Some fish _____ well in tanks.

**6** Last week the diver _____ a practice dive.

.......................................

Name

# K-W-L Chart

Write what you know about your topic. Next, write what you want to know. Then write what you have learned.

| What I **K**now | What I **W**ant to Know | What I Have **L**earned |
| --- | --- | --- |
|  |  |  |

Name

# Revising

Write your answers to these questions.

Did I check to make sure I wrote

my facts correctly? _____

Are there any facts I would like to add?

_____

_____

## Questions to Ask My Writing Partner

• What do you like best about my report?

• Is there anything you didn't understand?

• Have I told enough facts?

• What else would you like to know?

Name

# Making a Comic Book

Make your own incredible comic book.

**First, think of a story that is amazing but true—or mostly true.**

My comic book will be about:

_____

_____

**Use frames, or boxes, to tell your story. Use at least four frames. Write your idea for each frame.**

| Frame 1 | Frame 2 |
|---------|---------|
| Frame 3 | Frame 4 |

**Circle the numbers of two or three frames where you can add some fantastic details.**

**Now draw your comic book on two pieces of paper.**

## Check Your Work

- ☐ I drew an amazing story.
- ☐ My story has true details and fantastic details.
- ☐ I can explain which parts are true and which parts are made up.

Name

# Good News!

Cut out and paste the sentence parts in the
newspaper story in the order they happened.

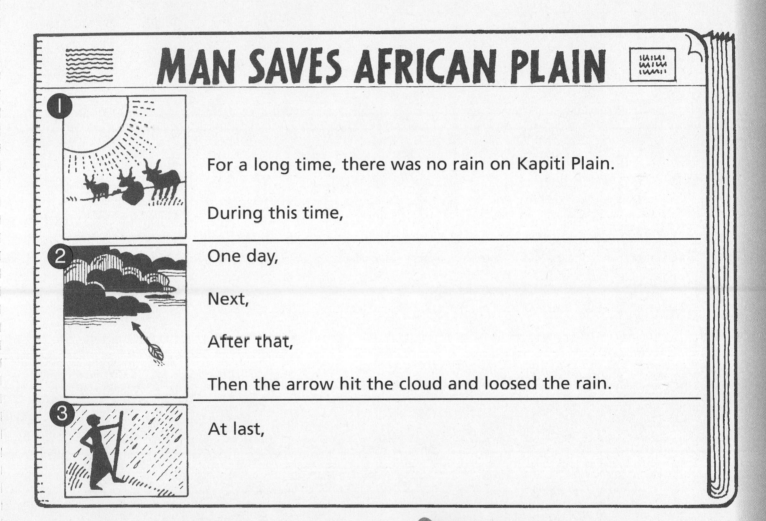

**MAN SAVES AFRICAN PLAIN**

1. For a long time, there was no rain on Kapiti Plain.

   During this time,

2. One day,

   Next,

   After that,

   Then the arrow hit the cloud and loosed the rain.

3. At last,

Ki-pat shot the arrow at the cloud.

the cows were hungry and dry.

the rain fell on the dry plain.

Ki-pat made an arrow from the feather.

an eagle dropped a feather.

Name _____

# Adding Endings

Write the base word and ending for each underlined word.

**1** The man was <u>named</u> Ki-pat.   _____  _____
base word          ending

**2** Ki-pat <u>looked</u> at the sky often.   _____  _____
base word          ending

**3** He was <u>hoping</u> for rain.   _____  _____
base word          ending

**4** An eagle <u>dropped</u> a feather.   _____  _____
base word          ending

**5** It had been <u>flapping</u> its wings.   _____  _____
base word          ending

Read each sentence.  Add **ed** or **ing** to the base word in ( ).
Write the new word to complete the sentence.

**6** Giraffes were _____ fast across the plain.  (run)

**7** Animals _____ to the river for a drink.  (race)

**8** The cows _____ for water.  (moo)

**9** Ki-pat was _____.  (smile)

**10** The rain _____ off the grass.  (drip)

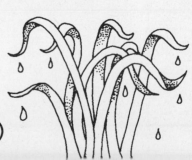

_____
Name

# Greetings!

Send this post card home from Kapiti Plain.  Use
words from the box to complete each sentence.
Write your name at the bottom of the card.

| wild |
| cloud |
| stood |
| happen |
| heavy |
| rain |
| change |

Dear Friends,

   The sky here is filled with a huge

_____.  But it is very dry here

because there is no _____.  All of the

_____ animals have gone away to look

for water.  I _____ on the plain all day

and did not see even one.  I hope that the weather will

_____ soon.  The animals may come

back if something will _____ to bring

a _____ rain.

                    Love,

Name

# Picture a Poem

**Cut out and paste the pictures in the boxes to complete
a poem.  Then read the poem aloud.  Listen for the rhyme.**

The [ ] was as dark as the [ ] .

The [ ] was bright like the [ ] .

The [ ] fell like [ ] .

A tropical storm had begun!

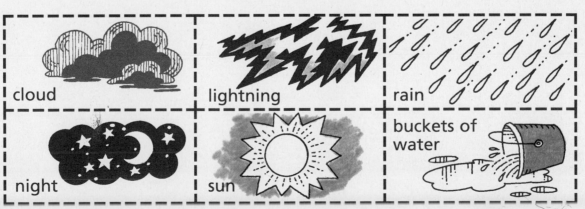

cloud

lightning

rain

night

sun

buckets of
water

Name

# From the Top

Look carefully at the picture.  Then color it.  Write
sentences to describe the picture from top to bottom.

_____

_____

_____

_____

_____

_____

Name _____

# Happy Endings

Each Spelling Word is made up of a base word and the ending **ed** or **ing**. The base word ends with a short vowel sound followed by a consonant. The final consonant in each base word is doubled before **ed** or **ing** is added.

drop + p + ed ➜ dropped
get + t + ing ➜ getting

## Spelling Words

1. **dropped**   5. **sitting**
2. **clapped**   6. **stepped**
3. **getting**   7. **hugging**
4. **stopped**   8. **shopping**

 Your Own Words

**Double the final consonant of the base word to finish each Spelling Word. Write the letter on the hut. Then write the words.**

1. clap _____ ed    3. hug _____ ing    5. shop _____ ing    7. get _____ ing

2. sit _____ ing    4. drop _____ ed    6. step _____ ed    8. stop _____ ed

1 _____    5 _____

2 _____    6 _____

3 _____    7 _____

4 _____    8 _____

**Which two Spelling Words have the short e sound in the base word?**

9 _____    10 _____

# Spelling Spree

Write Spelling Words to complete
the sentences in this play.

**Zebra:** Did you see what happened when it started to rain?

**Giraffe:** Children __(1)__ their hands and cheered.

**Eagle:** Farmers walked around kissing and __(2)__ their cows.

**Leopard:** The women who were __(3)__ for food __(4)__ their
bags on the ground and began to dance.

**Zebra:** People sure are funny!

**1** _____   **3** _____

**2** _____   **4** _____

Find and circle four Spelling Words that are spelled wrong
in this journal. Then write each word correctly.

**Tuesday**

My friend and I have just stept out of the hut.
The rain has finally stoped. The sky is gitting
lighter. A herd of cows is sittin in the tall grass.
Tomorrow I will look for my bow. I think I
dropped it near an acacia tree.

**5** _____

**6** _____

**7** _____

**8** _____

Name _____

# Big Plain

Write adjectives on the lines to describe the things in the picture.  Use the words from the box.

| | | |
|---|---|---|
| black | long | large |
| fresh | round | thin |

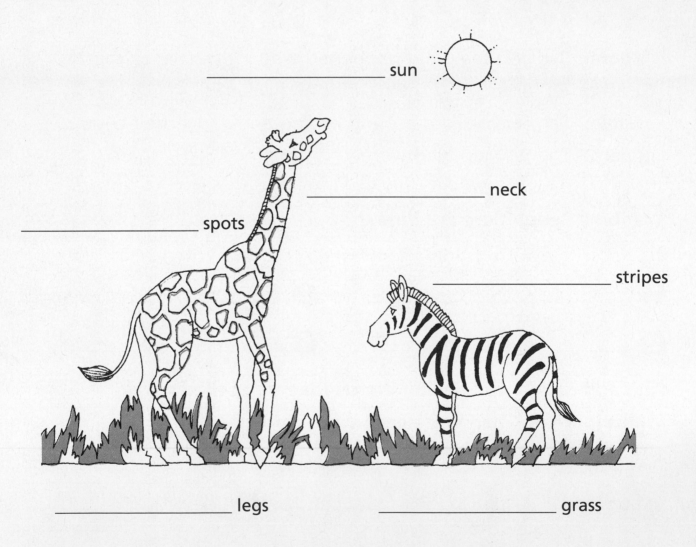

_____ sun

_____ neck

_____ spots

_____ stripes

_____ legs          _____ grass

Write a sentence about the picture.  Use two adjectives.

_____

_____

Name

# Step Right Up!

**Look at the drawing and follow the directions.**

1  Draw a circle around the birds that are identical.

2  Draw one line under what the magician has pulled out of the pot.

3  Draw a star next to the person who has just enough money.

4  Circle the person who has exactly twice as much as he needs.

5  Draw two lines under the person who is too poor to pay.

**Answer the questions.**

6  What would you double if you could? _____

7  How do you show that you're excited? _____

8  What is something most people do quickly? _____

.................
Name

# Mrs. Haktak's Diary

Complete the entries from Mrs. Haktak's
diary to tell about **Two of Everything**.

**Sunday**

I wish we weren't so _____.  The only food we

have comes from _____.

**Monday**

A lucky day!  Mr. Haktak found a magic _____ in the garden.

Whatever you put inside it _____!

So we kept putting in _____

_____.

**Tuesday**

Today was very strange.  I lost my balance and _____

_____.  First, Mr. Haktak

pulled me out, and then he pulled out _____

_____.  Next, Mr. Haktak

fell in, so now there are _____.

Name

# Matching Pairs

Draw a line from the event in the top row to the event that happens because of it in the bottom row.

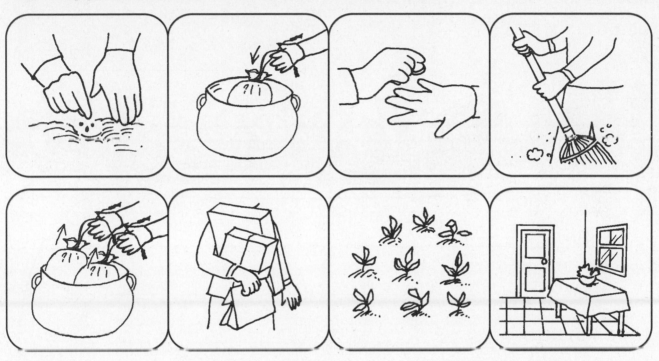

Complete each sentence so that it gives a cause and an effect.

| CAUSE | EFFECT |
|---|---|
| Mr. Haktak _____ seeds. | Plants _____. |
| Mr. Haktak pays _____. | He can _____ things. |
| Mrs. Haktak _____. | She has a _____ house. |
| Mrs. Haktak puts a _____ in the pot. | She has _____ purses. |

Name

# A Pot Full of Rhymes

Write a word from the box
that rhymes with each word in
the pot.

| boy | real | nose |
|------|-------|------|
| voice | noise | foil |
| royal | toast | join |

broil _____

coin _____

choice _____

joy _____

toys _____

loyal _____

Now write two sentences. In each sentence, use a word
from the pot.

_____

_____

_____

Name

# Interview with Mr. Haktak

**Choose words from the box to complete the questions.**

**Write the answers Mr. Haktak might give.**

| enough | person | poor | quickly |

**1** **Question:** What did you wish for when you were

_____? **Answer:**_____

_____.

**2** **Question:** How _____ did you

learn to pull things out of the pot? **Answer:** _____

_____.

**3** **Question:** Were you excited to see a _____

just like yourself? What did you say to him? **Answer:** _____

_____.

**4** **Question:** When you have _____

of everything, what will you do? **Answer:** _____

_____.

Name _____

# Big Pot, Little Pots

Read each sentence. Choose the word in the big pot that means almost the same thing as the underlined word. Write the word.

**1** Mr. Haktak <u>found</u> a magic pot in his garden. _____

**2** "The pot looks <u>old</u>," said Mr. Haktak. _____

**3** It was almost too <u>big</u> for him to carry home. _____

**4** Mrs. Haktak was <u>happy</u> with the pot. _____

**5** "We can <u>throw</u> coins into it," she

said. _____

large    discovered

ancient    delighted

toss

Read the word in each little pot and write a word that means almost the same.

tasty
_____

smart
_____

sleepy
_____

run
_____

choose
_____

# Seeing Double

**What would you like to have two of?  Draw pictures
of some things you would put in the pot.**

**Describe each thing you drew, using clear adjectives.**

_____

_____

_____

_____

_____

_____

Name

# Double or Nothing

Each Spelling Word has the vowel sound that you hear in **boy**. This vowel sound may be spelled **oi** or **oy**.

the vowel sound in boy ➜ coin, joy

**Write the missing letters to make Spelling Words. Then write each word on the purse that has the same spelling for the vowel sound in boy.**

sp ___ ___ l

b ___ ___ l

t ___ ___

___ ___ l

b ___ ___

c ___ ___ n

j ___ ___

j ___ ___ n

**oy**

1 _____

2 _____

3 _____

**oi**

4 _____

5 _____

6 _____

7 _____

8 _____

**Write Spelling Words to answer the questions.**

9 Which word begins and ends like **can**? _____

10 Which word begins like **speak**? _____

# Spelling Spree

Write a Spelling Word to finish each riddle. Then see if you can think of the answer to each riddle.

| Spelling Words | |
|---|---|
| 1. joy | 5. join |
| 2. coin | 6. boy |
| 3. oil | 7. spoil |
| 4. toy | 8. boil |

1. Why do we dress a baby _____ in blue?

2. Where would a fish put a gold _____?

3. What group did the rabbit _____ when it grew up?

4. Where can you always find a game or a _____?

1 _____

2 _____

3 _____

4 _____

Find and circle four Spelling Words that are spelled wrong in this note. Then write each word correctly.

Dear Mrs. Chang,

We are jumping for joi! Now nothing can spoile our fun. We did not find oyl in our yard. Instead we found a pot. We cannot boile water in it. But when we put one coin in the pot, we pull out two. We are rich!

Mr. and Mrs. Haktak

5 _____

6 _____

7 _____

8 _____

Riddle Answers:
1. because he can't dress himself
2. in a riverbank
3. the hare force
4. in the yellow pages

Name

# Boiling Over

Count the things in each pot.  Write an adjective that
tells how many.

**1** _____ coat

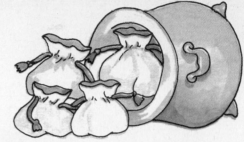

**4** _____ purses

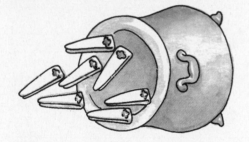

**2** _____ hairpins

**5** _____ hens

**3** _____ teapots

**6** _____ coins

Now write a sentence about what you would like to pull out
of the pot.  Use an adjective that tells **how many**.

**7** _____

_____

# Five-Senses Chart

Think of sense words to use in your description.
Write the words in the chart.

 Sight

 Sound

Smell

Taste

Feel

Name

# Check It Out!

**• Revising Checklist •**

Ask yourself these questions about your description.

☐ Do I use sense words to tell about how something looks, feels, tastes, sounds, or smells?

☐ Do I use details so that someone can picture it?

☐ Is there anything I want to add to my description?

_____

_____

_____

_____

## Questions to Ask My Writing Partner

• Can you picture what I am describing?

• Is there anything that is not clear?

• Is there anything I should add?

• What do you like best about my description?

Name

# A Great Gift

Cut out the shapes at the bottom of the page. Paste them where
they belong to tell the story. Write an ending to the story. Then
decorate the border around the story with different colors.

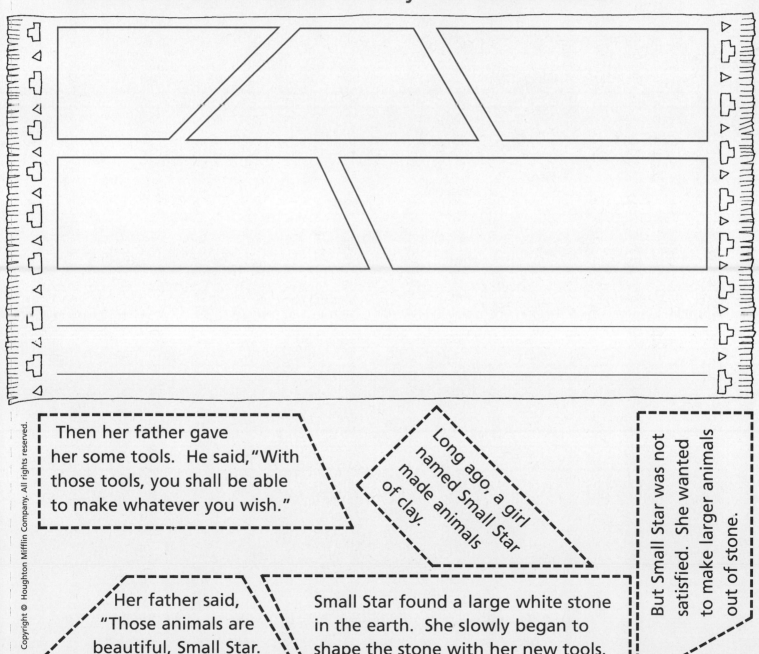

Then her father gave
her some tools. He said, "With
those tools, you shall be able
to make whatever you wish."

Long ago, a girl
named Small Star
made animals
of clay.

But Small Star was not
satisfied. She wanted
to make larger animals
out of stone.

Her father said,
"Those animals are
beautiful, Small Star.
You have a great gift."

Small Star found a large white stone
in the earth. She slowly began to
shape the stone with her new tools.

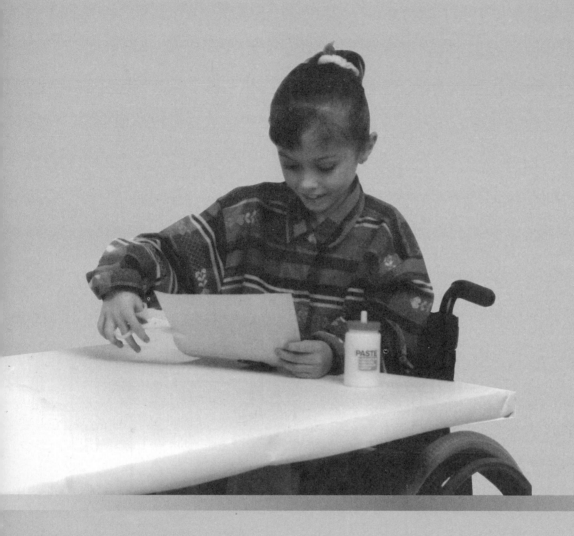

The Legend of the
Indian Paintbrush

**COMPREHENSION CHECK**

Name _____

# Hidden Message

## Use the clues to complete the puzzle.

**1** A Dream - _____ came to Little Gopher
when he went to the hills alone.

**2** The maiden showed Little Gopher a white _____ .

**3** Little Gopher painted scenes of great _____ and great deeds.

**4** He wanted to paint _____ that were bright and beautiful.

**5** Little Gopher found _____ filled with paint on the hillside.

**6** The brushes took root and became colorful _____ .

1. ____ ____ ____ ____ ____

2. ____ ____ ____ ____ ____ ____ ____

3. ____ ____ ____ ____ ____

4. ____ ____ ____ ____ ____ ____

5. ____ ____ ____ ____ ____

6. ____ ____ ____ ____

**Write the letters from the boxes to find out what Little Gopher**

**painted on the buckskin.** ____ ____ ____ ____ ____

Name _____

# What Will Little Gopher Do?

Read each page of Little Gopher's diary.
Think about what you know about him from
the story. Then answer each question.

The warriors asked me to go on the hunt today. It would be fun to go. But a voice in my dream told me to gather red berries to make paint.

**What do you think Little Gopher will do?**

_____

**Why do you think so?**

_____

_____

_____

_____

Last night the leader of our people had a Dream-Vision about talking to an eagle. He told me all about it.

**What do you think Little Gopher will do?**

_____

**Why do you think so?**

_____

_____

_____

_____

Name

# Painted Endings

Look at the base word on the brush and
the ending on the drop of paint. Put
them together to make a new word and
write it on a bowl. Cut and paste the
bowl under the paintbrush that matches.

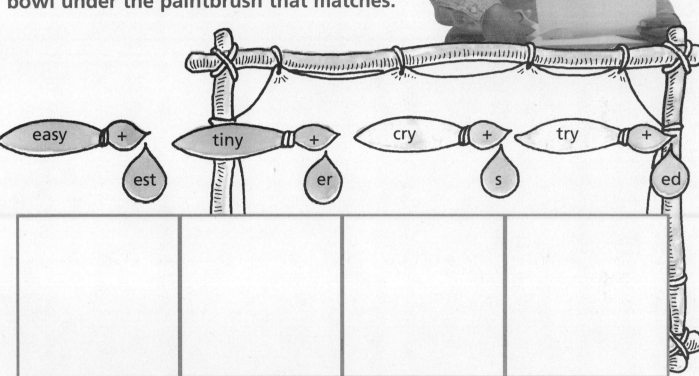

easy + est

tiny + er

cry + s

try + ed

On the back of this page, write two sentences. Use a word
from one of the bowls in each sentence.

→

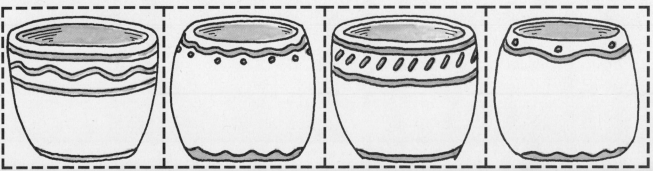

**Write two sentences.  Use a word from one of the bowls in each sentence.**

1 _____

_____

2 _____

_____

# A Legend

**Cut out the cloud shapes.  Paste the words where they belong.
On the back of this page, write an ending for the legend.**

Long _____, clouds were white from morning to night.
One day the clouds saw a rainbow.  They asked it, "May we use

_____ colors that make you so pretty?"
The rainbow said, "The colors do not belong to me.  You must
ask the sun."

So the clouds asked, "Sun, will you paint us with all the

_____ colors of the rainbow?"

The sun said, "Every morning, I paint the whole _____.

Wait until the end of the day.  I _____ see what colors I
have left."

The clouds waited.  When the day was nearly over, the sun

_____ painted clouds with red and purple, orange and gold.

| ago | earth | slowly | those | shall | different |

**Write an ending for the legend.**

And that is why

_____

_____

_____

_____

_____

_____

Name _____

# Better Word Pictures!

Look at the underlined action words.
Choose an adverb from the HOW
wheel that tells how the action
might happen.  Write the adverb in
the blank.

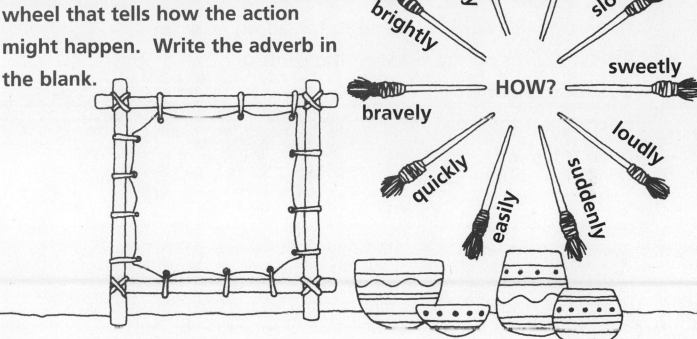

happily   carefully
brightly              slowly
                 sweetly
bravely   **HOW?**
                 loudly
quickly        suddenly
    easily

**1** Little Gopher <u>climbed</u> the mountain _____.

**2** The tiny birds <u>sang</u> _____.

**3** The wind <u>blew</u> _____.

**4** Little Gopher <u>saw</u> his Dream-Vision _____.

**5** He <u>walked</u> back to his village _____.

**6** Little Gopher <u>painted</u> the picture _____.

**7** The sunset <u>glowed</u> _____.

**8** Little Gopher <u>laughed</u> _____.

Name

# The Great Flower Contest

small, smaller, smallest    big, bigger, biggest

Imagine there was a contest to pick the prettiest
flower of all.  Write a legend to tell about how the
littlest flower on the hill won the contest.
Use **er** and **est** words
to compare things
in your legend.

_____

_____

_____

_____

_____

_____

_____

_____

*young, younger, youngest*   *happy, happier, happiest*

*pretty, prettier, prettiest*   *smart, smarter, smartest*

brave, braver, bravest    tall, taller, tallest

Name _____

# Paint a Picture

Each Spelling Word is made up of a base word and the ending **ed** or **ing**.  The base word has the vowel-consonant-**e** pattern.  The final **e** in the base word is dropped before **ed** or **ing** is added.

use – e + ed → used
make – e + ing → making

**Cross out the final e in each base word.  Then write a Spelling Word with the letters that are left.**

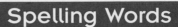

| | Spelling Words | |
|---|---|---|
| 1. | making | 5. placed |
| 2. | used | 6. shared |
| 3. | faded | 7. riding |
| 4. | taking | 8. liked |

 Your Own Words

1. take + ing   ① _____

2. like + ed   ② _____

3. ride + ing   ③ _____

4. use + ed   ④ _____

5. share + ed   ⑤ _____

6. make + ing   ⑥ _____

7. fade + ed   ⑦ _____

8. place + ed   ⑧ _____

**Which two Spelling Words have the long i sound in the base word?**

⑨ _____   ⑩ _____

# Spelling Spree

**Spelling Words**

1. making   5. placed
2. used     6. shared
3. faded    7. riding
4. taking   8. liked

**Write a Spelling Word for each clue.**

1. It rhymes with **hiding**.
   It begins like **rope**.

2. It rhymes with **raced**.
   It begins like **plant**.

3. It rhymes with **baking**.
   It begins like **time**.

4. It rhymes with **waded**.
   It begins like **fire**.

1 _____

2 _____

3 _____

4 _____

**Find and circle four Spelling Words that are spelled wrong in this
speech. Then write each word correctly.**

Little Gopher was a great artist. He was
always makeing beautiful things. He always shaired
them with the tribe.

He liket to watch the sun in the evening. Once he
painted a sunset. He uzed the brightest colors.
Even today the colors have not faded.

5 _____     7 _____

6 _____     8 _____

Name

# Ride a Painted Pony

Choose a word from the word box to finish each sentence.

fast

faster

fastest

The gray horse is fast.

1 The spotted horse is _____ than the gray horse.

2 The black horse is the _____ of all.

short

shorter

shortest

Russ is short.

3 Jimmy is _____ than Russ.

4 Willy is the _____ of the three boys.

Name

# Old Story, New Story

Tell an old story in a new way.  First, read this chart about **Two of Everything**.

| What happens | What makes it happen |
|---|---|
| Mr. and Mrs. Haktak find a pot. | Mr. Haktak digs it up. |
| They learn what the pot does. | One hairpin becomes two hairpins. |
| They use it to get what they want. | They put money in the pot. |
| Then they get two new people. | Mr and Mrs. Haktak fall into the pot. |
| At the end, everyone is happy. | They have everything they want. |

Now use the same ideas, in the same order, to tell your story.

| What happens | What makes it happen |
|---|---|
| My characters find | |
| They learn that it can | |
| They use it to | |
| Then | |
| At the end, | |

**Write your story.**
**Check your work.**

- ❏ My story is a new way of telling an old story.
- ❏ It keeps the same order of events.
- ❏ It tells why things happen the way they do.

# MY
# HANDBOOK

# Contents

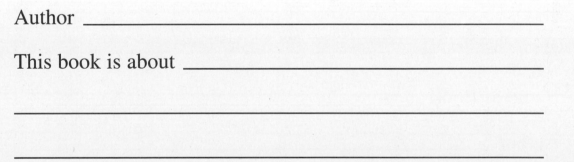

**Use this log to record the books you read on your own.**

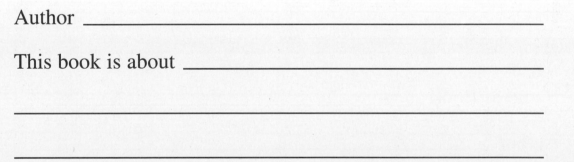

**MY READING LOG**

Name of Book _____

Author _____

This book is about _____

_____

_____

_____

Name of Book _____

Author _____

This book is about _____

_____

_____

_____

Name of Book _____

Author _____

This book is about _____

_____

_____

_____


Name of Book _____

Author _____

This book is about _____

_____

_____

_____


Name of Book _____

Author _____

This book is about _____

_____

_____

_____

Name of Book _____

Author _____

This book is about _____

_____

_____

_____

Name of Book _____

Author _____

This book is about _____

_____

_____

_____

Name of Book _____

Author _____

This book is about _____

_____

_____

_____

Name of Book _____

Author _____

This book is about _____

_____

_____

_____

Name of Book _____

Author _____

This book is about _____

_____

_____

_____

Name of Book _____

Author _____

This book is about _____

_____

_____

_____

Name of Book _____

Author _____

This book is about _____

_____

_____

_____

Name of Book _____

Author _____

This book is about _____

_____

_____

_____

Name of Book _____

Author _____

This book is about _____

_____

_____

_____

Name of Book _____

Author _____

This book is about _____

_____

_____


Name of Book _____

Author _____

This book is about _____

_____

_____


Name of Book _____

Author _____

This book is about _____

_____

_____

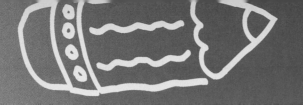

## Trace and write the letters.

Aa Aa

Bb Bb

Cc Cc

Dd Dd

Ee Ee

Ff Ff

Gg Gg

# HANDWRITING MODELS

Trace and write the letters.

*Hh Hh*

*Ii Ii*

*Jj Jj*

*Kk Kk*

*Ll Ll*

*Mm Mm*

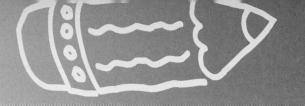

## HANDWRITING MODELS

**Trace and write the letters.**

*Nn Nn*

*Oo Oo*

*Pp Pp*

*Qq Qq*

*Rr Rr*

*Ss Ss*

*Tt Tt*

**Trace and write the letters.**

$\mathcal{Uu}$ $\mathcal{Uu}$

$\mathcal{Vv}$ $\mathcal{Vv}$

$\mathcal{Ww}$ $\mathcal{Ww}$

$\mathcal{Xx}$ $\mathcal{Xx}$

$\mathcal{Yy}$ $\mathcal{Yy}$

$\mathcal{Zz}$ $\mathcal{Zz}$

McDougal, Littell 1993 Handwriting

Trace and write the letters.

Aa Aa

Bb Bb

Cc Cc

Dd Dd

Ee Ee

Ff Ff

Gg Gg

# HANDWRITING MODELS

**Trace and write the letters.**

*Hh Hh*

*Ii Ii*

*Jj Jj*

*Kk Kk*

*Ll Ll*

*Mm Mm*

# HANDWRITING MODELS

**Trace and write the letters.**

Nn Nn

Oo Oo

Pp Pp

Qq Qq

Rr Rr

Ss Ss

Tt Tt

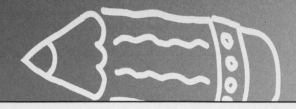

# HANDWRITING MODELS

**Trace and write the letters.**

*Uu Uu*

*Vv Vv*

*Ww Ww*

*Xx Xx*

*Yy Yy*

*Zz Zz*

## How to Study a Word

**1 LOOK at the word.**

- What does the word mean?
- What letters are in the word?
- Name and touch each letter.

**2 SAY the word.**

- Listen for the consonant sounds.
- Listen for the vowel sounds.

**3 THINK about the word.**

- How is each sound spelled?
- Close your eyes and picture the word.
- What other words have the same spelling patterns?

**4 WRITE the word.**

- Think about the sounds and the letters.
- Form the letters correctly.

**5 CHECK the spelling.**

- Did you spell the word the same way it is spelled in your word list?
- Write the word again if you did not spell it correctly.

# WORDS OFTEN MISSPELLED

**A**
again
already
any
are

**B**
been
believe
blue
both
bread
break
breakfast
brother
buy

**C**
come
could
country

**D**
do
does
doesn't
done
door

**E**
electric
eye

**F**
falling
feet
friend
from

**G**
give
glove
gone
great

**H**
half
have
head
helpful

**I**
I
isn't

**J**
judge
July

**K**
key

**L**
laugh
let's
live
lose
love
lying

**M**
many
money

**N**
neighbor
noise
no one
none
nothing

**O**
of
off

**P**
people
picnic
pretty

**Q**
quiet
quit

**R**
roar
rolling

**S**
said
sew
some

**T**
teeth
they
think
to
toe
too
two

**U**
until

**V**
voice

**W**
want
warm
was
wash
watch
what
who

**Y**
you
your

## *A Chair for My Mother*

**Vowel + r Sound in** car

vowel + r sound ⟶ j**ar**

⟶ **ar**m

### Spelling Words

1. jar
2. arm
3. hard
4. are
5. start
6. car
7. far
8. dark

### Challenge Words

1. apart
2. charcoal

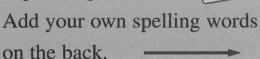

**My Study List**

Add your own spelling words on the back. ⟶

## *Clean Your Room, Harvey Moon!*

**The Vowel Sounds in**

moon **and** book

moon ⟶ n**oo**n

book ⟶ l**oo**k, f**oo**t

### Spelling Words

1. room
2. moon
3. book
4. soon
5. look
6. noon
7. broom
8. foot

### Challenge Words

1. cookie
2. cartoon

**My Study List**

Add your own spelling words on the back. ⟶

Name_____

 **My Study List**

1. _____

2. _____

3. _____

4. _____

5. _____

6. _____

7. _____

8. _____

### More Story Words

You may want to use these words in your own writing.

1. clean
2. done
3. few
4. notice
5. should
6. shout
7. today

Name_____

 **My Study List**

1. _____

2. _____

3. _____

4. _____

5. _____

6. _____

7. _____

8. _____

### More Story Words

You may want to use these words in your own writing.

1. brought
2. buy
3. fall
4. four
5. full
6. world

## Too Many Tamales

**Words That End with** er

bett**er**

broth**er**

ov**er**

### Spelling Words

1. better
2. after
3. over
4. under
5. mother
6. father
7. sister
8. brother

### Challenge Words

1. counter
2. center

**My Study List**

Add your own spelling words on the back. →

## Now One Foot, Now the Other

**Vowel + r Sound in** store

vowel + **r** sound → **for**

→ **m**o**re**

### Spelling Words

1. for
2. more
3. or
4. story
5. born
6. short
7. store
8. corn

### Challenge Words

1. before
2. morning

**My Study List**

Add your own spelling words on the back. →

Name _____

 **My Study List**

1. _____

2. _____

3. _____

4. _____

5. _____

6. _____

7. _____

8. _____

**More Story Words**

You may want to use these words in your own writing.

1. carried
2. mean
3. picture
4. warm
5. word
6. year

Name _____

 **My Study List**

1. _____

2. _____

3. _____

4. _____

5. _____

6. _____

7. _____

8. _____

**More Story Words**

You may want to use these words in your own writing.

1. laugh
2. light
3. nearly
4. second
5. white

## What Happened to Patrick's Dinosaurs?

**The Vowel Sound in** cow

ow ⟶ h**ow**, d**ow**n

ou ⟶ **ou**t, h**ou**se

### Spelling Words

1. how
2. out
3. now
4. house
5. down
6. brown
7. cow
8. mouse

### Challenge Words

1. about
2. shower

**My Study List**

Add your own spelling words on the back. ⟶

## The Day Jimmy's Boa Ate the Wash

**Words That End with**

s **or** es

s ⟶ trip**s**, face**s**

es ⟶ bus**es**, box**es**

### Spelling Words

1. trips
2. buses
3. classes
4. eggs
5. wishes
6. boxes
7. games
8. peaches

### Challenge Words

1. lunches
2. faces

**My Study List**

Add your own spelling words on the back. ⟶

Name_____

 **My Study List**

1._____

2._____

3._____

4._____

5._____

6._____

7._____

8._____

### More Story Words

You may want to use these words in your own writing.

1. cold
2. guess
3. later
4. leave
5. often

Name_____

 **My Study List**

1._____

2._____

3._____

4._____

5._____

6._____

7._____

8._____

### More Story Words

You may want to use these words in your own writing.

1. class
2. egg
3. farm
4. finally
5. hurry
6. sound

## Bringing the Rain to Kapiti Plain

**Words Ending in** ed **or** ing

clap + p + ed → clap**ped**

hug + g + ing → hug**ging**

### Spelling Words

1. dropped
2. clapped
3. getting
4. stopped
5. sitting
6. stepped
7. hugging
8. shopping

### Challenge Words

1. quitting
2. wrapped

## An Octopus Is Amazing

**The Vowel Sound in** ball

a → **a**ll, c**a**ll

**aw** → s**aw**, dr**aw**

### Spelling Words

1. all
2. call
3. draw
4. saw
5. small
6. ball
7. fall
8. paw

### Challenge Words

1. crawl
2. also

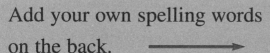

### My Study List

Add your own spelling words on the back. →

### My Study List

Add your own spelling words on the back. →

Name_____

 **My Study List**

1. _____

2. _____

3. _____

4. _____

5. _____

6. _____

7. _____

8. _____

## More Story Words

You may want to use these words in your own writing.

1. also
2. between
3. draw
4. eight
5. seven

Name_____

 **My Study List**

1. _____

2. _____

3. _____

4. _____

5. _____

6. _____

7. _____

8. _____

## More Story Words

You may want to use these words in your own writing.

1. change
2. cloud
3. happen
4. heavy
5. rain
6. stood
7. wild

# The Legend of the Indian Paintbrush

**More Words Ending in**
ed **or** ing
fade – e + ed → fad**ed**
use – e + ing → us**ing**

## Spelling Words

1. making
2. used
3. faded
4. taking
5. placed
6. shared
7. riding
8. liked

## Challenge Words

1. gazed
2. framed

**My Study List**
Add your own spelling words on the back. ➡

# Two of Everything

**The Vowel Sound in** boy
oy → t**oy**, j**oy**
oi → c**oi**n, sp**oi**l

## Spelling Words

1. joy
2. coin
3. oil
4. toy
5. join
6. boy
7. spoil
8. boil

## Challenge Words

1. voice
2. moist

**My Study List**
Add your own spelling words on the back. ➡

Name_____

 **My Study List**

1._____

2._____

3._____

4._____

5._____

6._____

7._____

8._____

## More Story Words

You may want to use these words in your own writing.

1. enough
2. excited
3. person
4. poor
5. pull
6. quickly

Name_____

 **My Study List**

1._____

2._____

3._____

4._____

5._____

6._____

7._____

8._____

## More Story Words

You may want to use these words in your own writing.

1. ago
2. different
3. earth
4. shall
5. slowly
6. those

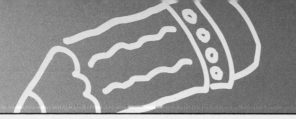

**1** A short vowel sound may be spelled **a, e, i, o,** or **u**.

hat    top
pet    fun
pin

**2** Two consonant sounds said close together may be spelled **st, tr, dr, gl, ft, sl,** or **ld**.

**st**ar    **gl**ad
**ju**st    le**ft**
**tr**ip    **sl**ip
**dr**ove    o**ld**

**3** The sound that begins **show** may be spelled **sh,** and the sound that ends **much** may be spelled **ch**.

**sh**e    **ch**in
wi**sh**    mu**ch**

**4** The sound that begins **when** may be spelled **wh**. The sounds that begin **thin** and **that** are both spelled **th**.

**wh**at    wi**th**
**th**ere

**5** The long **a** sound may be spelled **ai, ay,** or **a**-consonant-**e**.

tr**ai**n    m**a**d**e**
pl**ay**    g**a**m**e**

**6** The long **e** sound may be spelled **ee, ea,** or **e**-consonant-**e**.

t**ea**m    n**ee**d
r**ea**d    th**e**s**e**

**7** The long **o** sound may be spelled **oa, ow,** or **o**-consonant-**e**.

c**oa**t    h**o**m**e**
sl**ow**

**8** The long **i** sound may be spelled **i**-consonant-**e**.      s**ize**      l**ike**

**9** The long **u** sound may be spelled **u**-consonant-**e**.      **use**      c**ute**

**10** Words that end with **nd** have both the **n** and **d** sounds.      sa**nd**      **and**

**11** In words that end with **ng** or **nk**, you may not hear the **n** sound.      thi**ng**      ho**nk**

**12** In **contractions**, an apostrophe takes the place of a missing letter or letters.      you're   we'll      it's   don't

**13** Add **s** to most words to mean more than one. When a word ends with **s, x, sh,** or **ch,** add **es** to name more than one.      coat**s**   wi**shes**      bus**es**   pea**ches**      box**es**

**14** The final **e** in some words is dropped before adding **ed** or **ing.**      shar**ed**   tak**ing**

**15** The final consonant in some words is doubled before adding **ed** or **ing.**      stop**ped**   hug**ging**

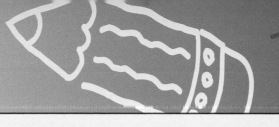

**16** The vowel sound in **ball** may be spelled **aw** or **a** before **ll.**   saw   call

**17** The vowel sound in **boy** may be spelled **oi** or **oy.**   **oi**l   joy

**18** The vowel sound in **cow** may be spelled **ow** or **ou.**   d**ow**n   m**ou**se

**19** The vowel + **r** sounds may be spelled **ar, or, ore,** or **er.**   **ar**m   st**ore**
born   ov**er**

**20** The vowel sound in **moon** may be spelled **oo.**   r**oo**m   s**oo**n

**21** The vowel sound in **book** may be spelled **oo.**   foot   look

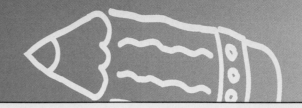

# Grammar, Capitalization, and Punctuation

## SENTENCES

A **sentence** tells what someone or something did.

    We ate dinner.                The boy rode the bus.

## Kinds of Sentences

A **telling sentence** tells something.  It begins with a capital letter.
It ends with a period.

    The horse won the race.        Cathy went to the store.

A **question** asks something.  It begins with a capital letter.
It ends with a question mark.

    Are you hungry?             Do you like to play soccer?

An **exclamation** shows strong feeling.  It begins with a capital letter.
It ends with an exclamation point.

    I loved that book!           What a fun day that was!

## Naming Parts and Action Parts

Every sentence has a **naming part** and an **action part.**

The **naming part** of a sentence tells who or what.

    **Jennifer** played in the snow.    **The sky** looks beautiful today.

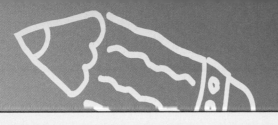

The **action part** of a sentence tells what is happening.

> The train **moves fast.**     Alex **laughs.**

## NOUNS

A **noun** names a person, a place, or a thing.

> The **girl** likes to run.     We saw the **pig**.
>
> Shelley went to the **park**.

## Special Nouns

Some nouns name special people, places, or things.

These **special nouns** begin with capital letters.

| Nouns | Special Nouns |
|---|---|
| My **dog** loves to play. | **Fluffy** loves to play. |
| The **park** is her favorite place. | **Jefferson Park** is her favorite place. |

## Nouns for One and More Than One

A noun can name one person, place, or thing.

> Tommy picked up the **cat**.     She walked by the **tree**.

A noun can also name more than one person, place, or thing.

> Tommy picked up the **cats**.     She walked by the **trees**.

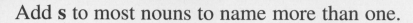

Add **s** to most nouns to name more than one.

The rug**s** were wet.          The hat**s** were silly.

Add **es** to nouns that end with **s, x, ch,** and **sh**
to name more than one.

These glass**es** are old.          The watch**es** need to be fixed.

The fox**es** were playing.          The dish**es** are dry.

A few nouns change their spelling to name more than one.

one child → two child**ren**          one man → two m**en**

one foot → two f**ee**t          one woman → two wom**en**

## PRONOUNS

A **pronoun** can take the place of a noun.

**He, she, it,** and **they** are pronouns.

**Karen** likes to swim.          **She** likes to swim.

**Brett** likes to swim too.          **He** likes to swim too.

**Maria and Brett** meet Karen          **They** meet Karen at the pool.
at the pool.

**The water** is very warm.          **It** is very warm.

## VERBS

A **verb** names an action.

> Mary **plays** the piano beautifully.
>
> The birds **fly** over the trees.
>
> The baby **drinks** the juice.
>
> I **get** my lunch.

### Verbs That Tell About Now

A verb can tell about an action that is happening now.

Add **s** to a verb that tells about one.

> The cat **plays** with the ball.      Tricia **smiles**.

Do not add **s** to a verb that tells about more than one.

> The boys **sing** songs.

### Verbs That Tell About the Past

A verb can name actions that happened before now, or in the past.

Add **ed** to a verb to show that something happened in the past.

> We **walked** to the store.
>
> Marta **called** her on the phone.
>
> Kim **rowed** the boat to safety.

## GRAMMAR GUIDE

### Is, Are, Was, Were

**Is** and **are** tell about something that is happening **now**.

Use **is** with one.  Use **are** with more than one.

Mr. Roberts **is** my teacher.         They **are** at home.

**Was** and **were** tell about something that happened in the past.

I **was** at the party yesterday.         My friends **were** already there.

### Irregular Verbs

Some special verbs change spelling to tell about the past.

### **Have** and **Do**

William **has** fun at the fair.         He **does** like hats.

People **have** fun at the fair.         They **do** like hats.

They **had** fun at the fair.         She **did** like hats.

### **Take** and **Make**

He **takes** some cookies.         He **makes** toys.

They **take** some cookies.         The girls **make** toys.

We **took** some cookies.         Everyone **made** toys.

### **Throw** and **Break**

Jimmy **throws** the ball.         The man **breaks** the glass.

The players **throw** the ball.         The workers **break** the glass.

Kara **threw** the ball.         The dog **broke** the glass.

## ADJECTIVES

An **adjective** is a word that tells how something looks, feels, tastes, smells, and sounds.

The **pretty** sunset made them happy. (looks)

The child was sleeping in a **soft** blanket. (feels)

The pizza was **spicy**. (tastes)

Many flowers have a **sweet** smell. (smells)

The **loud** siren scared her. (sounds)

Adjectives can also tell size, shape, color, and how many.

The **large** cloud moved slowly.   (size)

The child had a **round** face.    (shape)

The **blue** hat is in the box.  (color)

**Two** workers walked into the building.  (how many)

## Comparing with Adjectives

Add **er** to adjectives to compare two people, places, or things.

Lupe had **shorter** hair than Kelly.

Add **est** to compare more than two people, places, or things.

Lee had the **shortest** hair in the class.

## CAPITALIZATION

Every sentence begins with a capital letter.

    **T**he weather is sunny.

The names of the days of the week begin with capital letters.

    The party is on **T**uesday.

The names of months begin with capital letters.

    We go camping every year in **A**ugust.

The names of holidays begin with capital letters.

    I want to buy my mother a **M**other's **D**ay gift.

A title begins with a capital letter.

Put a period after **Mrs.**, **Mr.**, **Ms.**, and **Dr.**

The title **Miss** does not have a period.

| | | |
|---|---|---|
| **Mrs.** Jackson | **Ms.** Sloane | **Dr.** Lee |
| **Mr.** Fernandez | **Miss** Jones | |

The first word, the last word, and each important word in a book title begin with a capital letter. Book titles are underlined.

    I like the book <u>**B**ringing the **R**ain to **K**apiti **P**lain</u>.

## PUNCTUATION

### Ending Sentences

A telling sentence ends with a period.

> All of Timmy's friends will be at the party.

A question ends with a question mark.

> Will there be balloons and cake at the party?

An exclamation ends with an exclamation point.

> That cake was really good!

### Contractions

Use an apostrophe in contractions to take the place of missing letters.

| | |
|---|---|
| isn't (is not) | it's (it is) |
| can't (cannot) | I'm (I am) |
| wouldn't (would not) | they've (they have) |
| wasn't (was not) | they'll (they will) |
| we're (we are) | you're (you are) |

### Comma

Use a comma between the day and the year in dates.

> My sister was born August 22, 1995.

Use a comma between the name of a city and the name of a state.

> We went on a trip to Phoenix, Arizona.
>
> Her family lives in San Jose, California.

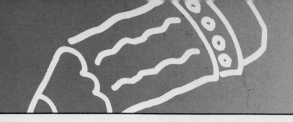

# PROOFREADING CHECKLIST

Read each question. Check your paper for each kind of mistake.
Correct any mistakes you find.

- ☐ Did I begin each sentence with a capital letter?
- ☐ Did I use the correct end mark?
- ☐ Did I spell each word correctly?
- ☐ Did I indent each paragraph?

## PROOFREADING MARKS

| | | |
|---|---|---|
| ∧ | Add one or more words. | want to<br>I ∧ see the play. |
| — | Take out one or more words.<br>Change the spelling. | The boat ~~did~~ moved slowly.<br>filled<br>The cloud ~~filed~~ the sky. |
| / | Make a capital letter a small letter. | The A̷nimals hid from the storm. |
| ≡ | Make a small letter a capital letter. | There are thirty days in april.<br>≡ |

| A | A | A | B | B | C | C | D | D |
|---|---|---|---|---|---|---|---|---|
| E | E | E | F | F | G | G | H | H |
| I | I | J | J | K | K | L | L | M |
| M | N | N | O | O | P | P | Q | Q |
| R | R | S | S | T | T | U | U | V |
| V | W | W | X | X | Y | Y | Z | Z |

fold

fold

fold

| d | d | c | c | b | b | a | a | a |
| h | h | g | g | f | f | e | e | e |
| m | l | l | k | k | j | j | i | i |
| q | q | p | p | o | o | n | n | m |
| v | u | u | t | t | s | s | r | r |
| z | z | y | y | x | x | w | w | v |

fold

fold

fold

| TOO MANY TAMALES | NOW ONE FOOT, NOW THE OTHER | A CHAIR FOR MY MOTHER | CLEAN YOUR ROOM, HARVEY MOON! |
|---|---|---|---|
| High-Frequency Words | High-Frequency Words | High-Frequency Words | High-Frequency Words |
| laugh | carried | brought | clean |
| ? | ? | ? | ? |
| light | mean | buy | done |
| ? | ? | ? | ? |
| nearly | picture | fall | few |
| ? | ? | ? | ? |
| second | warm | four | notice |
| ? | ? | ? | ? |
| white | word | full | should |
| ? | ? | ? | ? |
|  | year | world | shout |
| ? | ? | ? | ? |
|  |  |  | today |
| ? | ? | ? | ? |
|  |  |  |  |
| ? | ? | ? | ? |
|  |  |  |  |
| ? | ? | ? | ? |
|  |  |  |  |
| ? | ? | ? | ? |

| CLEAN YOUR ROOM, HARVEY MOON! Spelling Words | A CHAIR FOR MY MOTHER Spelling Words | NOW ONE FOOT, NOW THE OTHER Spelling Words | TOO MANY TAMALES Spelling Words |
|---|---|---|---|
| room | jar | for | better |
| ? | ? | ? | ? |
| moon | arm | more | after |
| ? | ? | ? | ? |
| book | hard | or | over |
| ? | ? | ? | ? |
| soon | are | story | under |
| ? | ? | ? | ? |
| look | start | born | mother |
| ? | ? | ? | ? |
| noon | car | short | father |
| ? | ? | ? | ? |
| broom | far | store | sister |
| ? | ? | ? | ? |
| foot | dark | corn | brother |
| ? | ? | ? | ? |
| cookie | apart | before | counter |
| ? | ? | ? | ? |
| cartoon | charcoal | morning | center |
| ? | ? | ? | ? |

| AN OCTOPUS IS AMAZING | WHAT HAPPENED TO PATRICK'S DINOSAURS? | THE DAY JIMMY'S BOA ATE THE WASH |
|---|---|---|
| High-Frequency Words | High-Frequency Words | High-Frequency Words |
| also | cold | class |
| ? | ? | ? |
| between | guess | egg |
| ? | ? | ? |
| draw | later | farm |
| ? | ? | ? |
| eight | leave | finally |
| ? | ? | ? |
| seven | often | hurry |
| ? | ? | ? |
|  |  | sound |
| ? | ? | ? |
|  |  |  |
| ? | ? | ? |
|  |  |  |
| ? | ? | ? |
|  |  |  |
| ? | ? | ? |

| THE DAY JIMMY'S BOA ATE THE WASH<br>Spelling Words | WHAT HAPPENED TO PATRICK'S DINOSAURS?<br>Spelling Words | AN OCTOPUS IS AMAZING<br>Spelling Words |
| --- | --- | --- |
| trips | how | all |
| ? | ? | ? |
| buses | out | call |
| ? | ? | ? |
| classes | now | draw |
| ? | ? | ? |
| eggs | house | saw |
| ? | ? | ? |
| wishes | down | small |
| ? | ? | ? |
| boxes | brown | ball |
| ? | ? | ? |
| games | cow | fall |
| ? | ? | ? |
| peaches | mouse | paw |
| ? | ? | ? |
| lunches | about | crawl |
| ? | ? | ? |
| faces | shower | swallow |
| ? | ? | ? |

| THE LEGEND OF THE INDIAN PAINTBRUSH | TWO OF EVERYTHING | BRINGING THE RAIN TO KAPITI PLAIN |
| :---: | :---: | :---: |
| High-Frequency Words | High-Frequency Words | High-Frequency Words |
| ago | enough | change |
| ? | ? | ? |
| different | excited | cloud |
| ? | ? | ? |
| earth | person | happen |
| ? | ? | ? |
| shall | poor | heavy |
| ? | ? | ? |
| slowly | pull | rain |
| ? | ? | ? |
| those | quickly | stood |
| ? | ? | ? |
| | | wild |
| ? | ? | ? |
| ? | ? | ? |
| ? | ? | ? |

| BRINGING THE RAIN TO KAPITI PLAIN | TWO OF EVERYTHING | THE LEGEND OF THE INDIAN PAINTBRUSH |
|---|---|---|
| Spelling Words | Spelling Words | Spelling Words |
| dropped | joy | making |
| ? | ? | ? |
| clapped | coin | used |
| ? | ? | ? |
| getting | oil | faded |
| ? | ? | ? |
| stopped | toy | taking |
| ? | ? | ? |
| sitting | join | placed |
| ? | ? | ? |
| stepped | boy | shared |
| ? | ? | ? |
| hugging | spoil | riding |
| ? | ? | ? |
| shopping | boil | liked |
| ? | ? | ? |
| quitting | voice | gazed |
| ? | ? | ? |
| wrapped | moist | framed |

| | | |
|---|---|---|
| second | full | clean |
| white | world | done |
| class | carried | few |
| egg | mean | notice |
| farm | picture | should |
| finally | warm | shout |
| hurry | word | today |
| sound | year | brought |
| cold | laugh | buy |
| guess | light | fall |
| later | nearly | four |

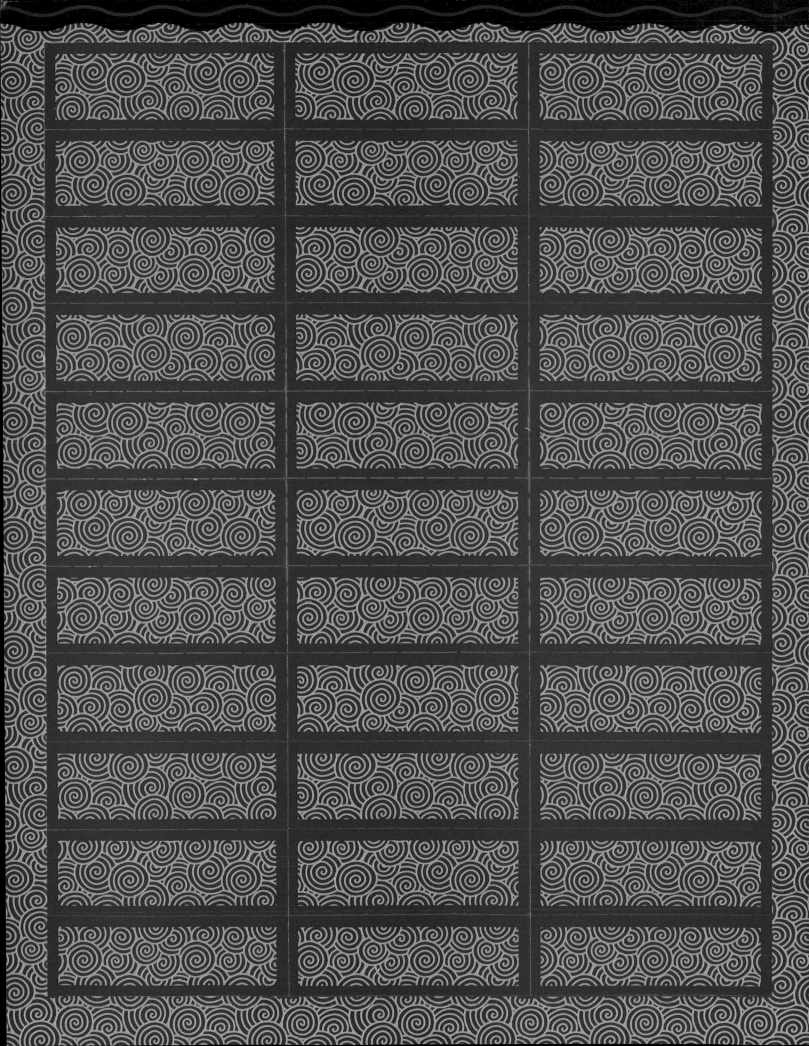

| | | |
|---|---|---|
| earth | rain | leave |
| shall | stood | often |
| slowly | wild | also |
| those | enough | between |
| | excited | draw |
| | person | eight |
| | poor | seven |
| | pull | change |
| | quickly | cloud |
| | ago | happen |
| | different | heavy |

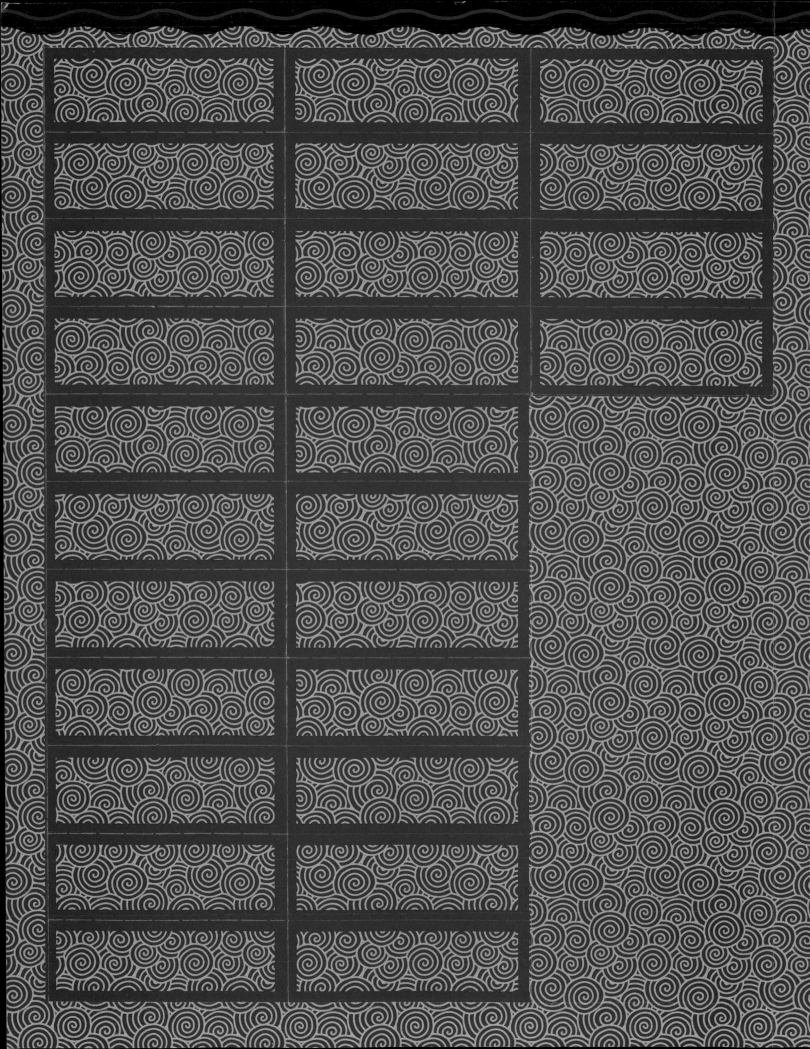